Peace Of Mind

Messages of Hope
for a Troubled World

Harold C. Warlick, Jr.
Dean of the Chapel
High Point University
High Point, North Carolina

Foreword by Bob Timberlake

Peace Of Mind

Messages of Hope for a Troubled World

Copyright ©2010 Harold C. Warlick, Jr.

All Scripture verses are taken from the New Revised Standard Version Bible,
copyright 1990, Division of Christian Education of the National Council of
Churches of Christ in the United States of America. Used by permission.

Cover photo is from the painting, "May" an original 11 ¼″ x 16 ¼″ watercolor by
Bob Timberlake, Part of *The Bob Timberlake Collection*, The Riverwood Press, Inc.,
Lexington, NC, 1977. Used by permission of Bob Timberlake, Inc.
Quote from Charles Kuralt in introduction, used by permission of Bob Timberlake, Inc.
Originally published in *The Bob Timberlake Collection*, page 142.

For more information, contact:
High Point University Press
833 Montlieu Avenue
High Point, NC 27262
(336) 841-9201
www.highpoint.edu

Library of Congress Catalog Number in Publication Data
ISBN: 978-0-9770555-6-2
Printed in the United States of America

— *acknowledgements* —

The production of any book requires the pulling together of many people for thought-provoking feedback, meticulous editorial work, laborious proofreading and constant encouragement. When one produces, in book form, messages that were delivered orally to diverse audiences over a period of time, the work can prove to be doubly challenging. Consequently, I owe a special thanks to Shannon LeFever, Manager of Chapel Programs, at High Point University. Her keen eye, attention to detail, and gentle persuasiveness enabled me to finish this writing project with mind and emotions mostly intact. Her proofing and editing skills are of the highest order. Dr. Bobby Hayes, Assistant Professor of English, meticulously read and edited the manuscript.

My deep appreciation is extended to my friend Bob Timberlake. He listens and informs as well as he paints and talks, no small feat. His willingness to allow the use of one of his paintings for the cover and his heartfelt and articulate foreword far exceeded any reasonable expectation.

Robert Blocker and Mary Ann Akers are long-time friends, whose friendship and professional feedback has been especially valuable. Robert is a world treasure in his field and enhances the lives of many from his perch as Dean of The School of Music at Yale University. Mary Ann and husband, Michael, have recently brought into the world their son, Zach. In the midst of tremendous responsibilities, domestic and professional, she made time to offer encouragement and respond to the manuscript.

The work of the all-student Board of Stewards at High Point

University has for over two decades helped create a vibrant and packed venue for worship services in the Charles E. Hayworth Sr. Chapel at the University. In like manner, the Official Board of Blowing Rock Methodist Church, Blowing Rock, North Carolina, capably chaired by Charles Fonville, has helped create the same in that seasonal church.

Nido R. Qubein, President of High Point University, and Rosemary Keller of H. Thomas Keller and Associates in High Point provided valuable resources and support that enabled this attractive volume to be produced.

I have been fortunate to have many who have watered my seeds of life for decades, in ways spiritual and challenging. Their support, critique and encouragement have enriched me beyond measure. Foremost among these has been my wife, Diane, who has listened to all of these messages and many more. It is to her that this volume is dedicated.

Foreword

I am nothing but a piece of fabric, and whatever I've become or will be, is all because of my family, and the places, things and people with which I have crossed paths. I am woven into that piece of fabric by all of these influences and experiences, and most have been wonderful and helpful.

Having grown up in the Methodist Church for these 73 years, and especially in the most formative years of my early life, I felt, and continue to feel, a comfort in church that I don't feel anywhere else (except maybe sometimes in nature). It is a feeling of being protected, safe, comfortable, and at peace. I feel good about myself when I'm in church. I feel a sense of accomplishment, self-esteem, and self-confidence. I don't quite know exactly why, but it makes me feel good, simple as that.

Early Sunday School teachers, my preachers, past and present, dinners on the church grounds, chicken pie suppers, and church friends have all touched me. As a teenager, I was fortunate to have a minister, Howard C. Wilkinson, who was my very good friend, as well as my fishing and hunting partner. He later performed Kay's and my wedding ceremony, as well as the weddings of all three of our children. I learned much from him in church, in duck blinds, and on lakes fishing.

My grandfather, Emery E. Raper, whom I never knew, was setting my table before I was born. I have been influenced by him through word of mouth from such folks as Senator Sam Ervin, Jr, and others, by his writings, by his involvement with the Methodist Church, and by helping others. His help to establish and open High Point University in the 1920's has always fascinated me, and through High Point, I've grown to know and respect Dr. Hal Warlick. We have become good friends.

And as I've grown older and maybe a little wiser, I've been fortunate enough to come across my very interesting and very intelligent new "preacher" friend, Dr. Warlick, in another venue. Kay and I spend part of our summertimes in our wonderful North Carolina mountains, and this is where I really get to know this fellow who makes me feel better, more content, and more comfortable in his little mountain Methodist Church in Blowing Rock, North Carolina. This guy speaks my language; he preaches with the Bible in one hand and the newspaper of today in the other, remembering our heritage and uniting my heart with his heart. He makes me think, bringing forth profound questions of today, in ways that often pull me back to the memories of yesterday—as Charles Kuralt told me over and over, "about a time when people lived further apart—but closer together." He makes me relive and remember the quotes and sayings that have meant so much to me over the years. The simple early, "Don't tell lies" and "Don't sell what you don't own" and other truisms remind me of lessons I learned in Sunday school many years ago.

I sit mostly in the back of the historic old mountain church during the summer months, with my better three-fourths, Kay, and I always get recharged by Hal's sermons, even when I'm having a tough time or feeling rough. He pulls me into positive thinking. "Just when the caterpillar thought the world was over—it became a butterfly." I know all this sounds pretty simple, but it happens to me. Even with my very complicated life, I am constantly reminded there are only three things anyone needs to be happy: something to look forward to, something worthwhile to work hard at, and someone to love.

I guess I'm saying that Hal Warlick's sermons and our talks together reinvigorate me; they rekindle my creative juices and faith in the positive, while bringing me down to earth by remembering my forefathers and all those who have given so much to make me who I am and who make possible all that I do.

On many a Sunday in Hal's church, I remember the old saying by a fairly new writer friend, Mike Gaddis, "Remember this day, Boy, as it has been, for in this way, it can never be again." This makes me appreciate and live every day to the fullest. I get recharged by going to church, and I really get a jolt by listening to my friend, Hal Warlick—it's better than Gatorade.

"You sometimes have to listen hard to hear the beat of butterfly wings." Hal makes you want to listen harder and want to hear more—even after the crowd has left the building.

Bob Timberlake

Introduction

The spring of the year in general, and the month of May in particular, are pivotal times in my existence. My vocation's task is to try to preach about God in the midst of our human hopes and fears. My church audiences are composed almost exclusively of either college students or older adults. The former pack the chapel at High Point University for services during fall, winter and spring, while the latter make their way during the summer months to a 110-year-old seasonal church located in the mountain village of Blowing Rock, North Carolina. Both audiences have more in common than casual observers might think. Consequently, both are receptive to timeless images of hope and courage that can inspire us, as human beings, to constantly seek to experience and retain the peace of mind that is promised in scriptures.

The month of May forms an axis or linchpin in that endeavor for both audiences. Each May, the older folks, me included, turn our thoughts to seashores, mountains, and lakes. Images of summers past and the summer to come find their way into the fertile grounds of the memories and imaginations of us seasoned veterans of life.

May, likewise, provides a linchpin for many young people.

Some will be preparing to graduate from high school and leave the
security of home to enter the college experience. Others will be
preparing to graduate from college, leaving behind the comfort of
having lived in an environment populated by people their own age,
and entering an uncertain world of work, potential joblessness, and
immense financial responsibilities. In my world, May is a time when
old and young friends alike must summon what modern theologian
Paul Tillich so clearly described as "the courage to be," and what
Jesus of Nazareth so clearly promised as the "peace" that is different
from what humans call peace.

It is symbolic and appropriate, then, that the cover of this book
contains the beautiful painting by Bob Timberlake titled, "May."
The inspiring portrait is rich with images from nature and religion—images of peace, courage, and hope. The leftover orange and
brown leaves of winter are giving way to the green grass and blue
wildflowers of spring that are coming up through the forest floor.
The robin's egg has hatched, and the baby bird has taken flight to
begin its new life. The words of Charles Kuralt that accompanied
this painting when it was first published illuminate this miracle that
takes place each year:

> Spring was for sitting down in the moist pine
> needles, studying a patch of forest floor; and seeing
> the universe down there in a robin's egg, moss, and
> bluets. Spring was the nameless yearning of sitting
> there, feeling the weak sun on your shoulders,
> feeling reborn amid so much rebirth.

Human experiences of being reborn amid much rebirth
happen often. I have seen them, and so have you. One summer
Sunday in Blowing Rock, as the worship service was about to start,
the wife of a retired faculty member at High Point University led
her mother up the stone walk to the entrance of our church on
Main Street. She introduced her mother as Martha Howell Guess
and said, "I finally got mother up here from her home in Denmark,
South Carolina. Mother has wanted to get *back* to this church." The

head usher and I offered to take her mother down to the front of the church, but Mrs. Guess said that she wanted to sit out on the porch, look through the open doors, and take everything in. We produced a chair, and Mrs. Guess sat there, all by herself. She said, "I want to sit here with the sun on my shoulders where I can see the church yard, look down the aisles, see all the people, and hear the service. I want to see and hear it all."

I maintained eye contact with her from my vantage point in the pulpit area throughout much of the service. She was beaming and appeared to be literally feeding herself, spiritually and physically, from the service. At the end of the service, she was ecstatic. I was stunned to learn that the last time she had been at the church was 75 years earlier. She said, "Yes, it was 1932, and my grandmother brought me. I was 12 years old, and now I am 87."

She said she sat on our porch that day to also watch the light stream in through the windows. The church didn't have windows or heating when she had last attended. It was always dark and cold. But it had been there for her in times of need. Her mother had died when Martha was but two days old. The infant child was taken in by her grandmother. As the child grew, she and her grandmother came to the Blowing Rock Methodist Church, when it was open. But in 1932, the church was only able to open four Sundays. The next year, the church was abandoned and stayed closed for 15 years, during which time Martha moved away. She grew up, married, and had children, grandchildren, and great grandchildren of her own. For 75 years, she kept in her heart the joy of her childhood. For 75 years, she wanted to get back to where God was first real for her. She truly was sitting on the church porch that day, being reborn amid so many rebirths. Something old was becoming something new for her.

Being reborn amid much rebirth happens all the time. It is what my wife, Diane, can do to make plants grow and flowers blossom up through the hard sand rock of Guilford County, North Carolina; it is what Bob Timberlake can bring to life with a brush, some paint and a canvas; it is what Robert Blocker can create in sound and finesse from a piano keyboard; it is what the good teacher can bring to illumination from the mind of a willing and receptive student; it is what the good carpenter can build out of the rawest of materials; it is what the good preacher can craft with but a few words from sacred scripture to inspire others; it is what the good farmer can bring out of the ground to share with neighbors and eliminate their hunger, as well as their loneliness. But best of all, it is what the good Creator God can do for all God's children, by leading them to that place where there will be no more tears, no more sorrows, no more pain, no more war, and no more injustice—a place where it will be eternal spring, and where we children of God will be reborn amid so much rebirth from those who arrive after us. That knowledge is for me, peace of mind.

Jesus told us that if we have seen Him, then we have seen God, because God is love. The Scriptures tell us nothing about Jesus' physical appearance except for one clue: to a faithful follower named Mary Magdalene, he looked more like a gardener than anything else on earth. And we know what a good gardener does: plant, water and nourish the seeds, flowers, and shrubs so they can grow as strong and beautiful as they can be. Essentially, my preaching is an attempt to put together stories, Scriptures, and interpretations. Its purpose is to enable listeners to encounter some of the experiences, themes, and images that have watered and nourished my little seeds of hope and trust into a larger and stronger peace of mind. I hope that for you, the reader, some of your encounters with the messages that follow will nourish your own seeds, help you to grow, and strengthen your own peace of mind. Take what you like.

—Hal Warlick
Dean of the Chapel
High Point University

Contents

PART IV—A HORSE OF A DIFFERENT COLOR

PART V—PEACE OF MIND

PART I

— Forces to be Reckoned With —

Role Reversal

—— *the lessons* ——

*But when Christ had offered for all time a single sacrifice for sins, "he
sat down at the right hand of God," and since then has been waiting
"until his enemies would be made a footstool for his feet." For by a single
offering he has perfected for all time those who are sanctified. And the
Holy Spirit also testifies to us, for after saying, "This is the covenant that
I will make with them after those days, says the Lord: I will put my laws
in their hearts, and I will write them on their minds," he also adds, "I
will remember their sins and their lawless deeds no more." Where there is
forgiveness of these, there is no longer any offering for sin.*

—Hebrews 10:12-18

*An account of the genealogy of Jesus the Messiah, the son of David, the
son of Abraham. Abraham was the father of Jacob, and Jacob the father
of Judah and his brothers, and Judah the father of Perez and Zerah
by* **Tamar**, *and Perez the father of Hezron, and Hezron the father of
Aram, and Aram the father of Aminadab, and Aminadab the father of
Nahshon, and Nahshon the father of Boaz by* **Rahab**, *and Boaz the
father of Obed by* **Ruth**, *and Obed the father of Jesse, and Jesse the
father of King David.*

And David was the father of Solomon by **the wife of Uriah**, *and
Solomon the father of Rehoboam, and Rehoboam the father of Abijah,
and Abijah the father of Asaph.*

—Matthew 1:1-7

y predecessor as minister of Emerywood Baptist Church in High Point was Leon Hollingsworth. He came to that church from Wake Forest University, where he had been chaplain for 22 years. My first week at the church, he visited me. He told me that he had recently gone on a trip to the mountains. He was driving five miles per hour over the speed limit, and he got pulled for speeding. As the blue light from the highway patrol car flashed in his rearview mirror, the churning in his stomach was exceeded only by his anger. Putting on his best professional face and a humble demeanor, he gave the officer the requested information and jotted in his date book the time and location of his court appointment.

On the appointed day, he journeyed to the county seat town in the mountains, armed with a notebook full of excuses to try and impress the judge into letting this important man of the cloth out of his speeding ticket. His face turned an ashen gray as the proceedings began. The judge who walked into the room and took his center stage seat was a former political science major at Wake Forest. Twenty years earlier, Hollingsworth had given him a failing grade in a freshman religion course. With timidity, the preacher approached the bench. "I'm not going to get out of this, am I?" he meekly asked. The reply that came from the judge was "Not a chance!" That's a role reversal.

Role reversals tend to catch us by surprise. The letter to the Hebrews suggests that most of the Jewish people who had been raised in the temple cult and attended that temple without fail on the Sabbath were shocked at the role reversal they experienced in Jesus. This Jesus, who attacked the temple and its priests, is pictured in the letter as having become the High Priest whose sacrifice (his bodily death) makes everyone holy. This vagabond Jesus, born in little Bethlehem and raised in the backwater town of Nazareth, has become the high priest.

Albert Schweitzer saw Jesus of Nazareth as one who threw himself on the great wheel of history, determined to show humanity the kingdom of love and forgiveness that was lying crushed and lost within our social institutions.

In his book *Dear Mr. Brown*, Harry Emerson Fosdick told of a father's desperate attempt to explain the nature of God to his young daughter, who was confused by the stories of war and destruction in the early part of the Old Testament. The father read from the *later* prophets: "What does the Lord require of you but to do justice, and to love kindness, and to walk humbly with your God?" Then he read from the New Testament: "Beloved, let us love one another, for love is of God, and he who loves is born of God and knows God." Presently, the little girl responded thoughtfully: "Daddy, God grew better as he got older, didn't he?" That's one way of putting it. Another way is to say that God grows "better" as humans grow into a more mature knowledge of God's love and forgiveness.[1]

The corridors of time are crowded with men and women, laboring under the weight of the laws of the world and their own insensitive and stupid past experiences. Each awaits an appearance before the high priest, the judge of their existence. Each has in hand the personal accumulations of a lifetime, hoping little offerings of money, some understanding, and valuable trinkets and accomplishments will sustain them.

I can imagine us all one day, having been personally "flashed down" on the highway of life, yet trying to remain serene and controlled in the face of it all. We will probably thumb through our excuses, our offerings, our lists of good deeds, and our scraps of Scriptures, hoping the hearing before our ultimate judge will go well.

The great high priest glances down. "Don't need your offerings, though they helped your spirit," he calmly states. "Don't need your Christian music, though I enjoyed listening to it, and it expanded your spirituality," he continues. "Don't need your scraps of Scriptures, though I am glad you memorized them," he adds. "Don't need your list of good deeds, though human need demanded them," he concludes.

From a worldly perspective, things do not often look great for us before the judge. Many are familiar with the name Alexis De Tocqueville. There are all kinds of people who proudly trumpet their Americanism as members of the Alexis De Tocqueville Society. De Tocqueville spent nine months in America in 1831 and wrote two fat volumes admiring the entrepreneurial spirit of the American people and how they formed a polished society moderated by common values, civic pride, and religious observance. That was all well and good. But just nine years later, he reversed himself and wrote that American life was dominated by people who lacked moderation. His exact words to Americans were these: "What is certain is that, for some years, you have strangely abused the advantages given to you by God."[2]

That was then, and this is now. As we stand before the high priest in our day, we complain that we are hurting. But it is all relative. We are still quite self-indulgent, free and wealthy on a world scale, and have no real competition as a society when it comes to being blessed by God. China's people still labor under an authoritarian government that represses freedoms at every turn. And 40 percent of India's people are illiterate. In fact, 1,000 Indian children die of diarrheal sickness every day, over 365,000 children a year. An estimated 700 million Indians have no access to a toilet. We don't have any competition when it comes to the blessings we Americans have received and are still receiving from God.

We still have the blessings and the entrepreneurial spirit. Our biggest company, Wal-Mart, was founded in only 1962, and Google was conceived in a California college dorm room only 13 years ago. When it comes to entrepreneurships, we have got it, and we will get it again. But when we look at the rest of the world—we have much to answer for. To quote De Tocqueville, we have certainly abused the advantages given to us by God. We twenty-first century speeders through life, each and every one of us, stand before the ultimate High Priest, and our plaintive question shivers its way to the fore-front: "I'm not going to get out of this, am I?"

According to the Scriptures, the response from the high priest reverberates its way across the corridors of time and the wreckage of human frailty—"Of course you are going to get out of this. I took all I had, even my life, and sacrificed it for you. I got the charges dropped, and I paid the ticket for you. I have erased the record. Now, you get your act together and love your neighbor and the people in this world like I have loved you." We twenty-first century speeders through life stand before a High Priest who has already paid our ticket for us. This is, indeed, good news. There is a wonderful old gospel song called "Jesus Dropped The Charges." The O'Neal twins, two fabulous black singers, the last of whom died only last year, made it famous. It is a rousing song with incredible lyrics:

> "I was guilty of all the charges, doomed and disgraced,
> but Jesus with His special love, saved me by His grace;
> He pleaded and He pleaded, He pleaded my case.
> Jesus dropped the charges, Jesus dropped the charges,
> and now I'm saved through faith and grace."

The genealogy of Jesus, as presented in his family tree accord-ing to Matthew's gospel, says it all. The Jews did not particularly like women being in high places in Old Testament times; but neither did Americans prior to the 1900's. Women didn't get the right to vote until 1920 here. So it is surprising to find four women listed in the family tree of Jesus, especially since Matthew took great pains to run the genealogy back through Jesus' father to Abraham. These four women had only two things in common: they were all foreigners to Israel, and they were all involved in slanderous activities.

Tamar was a prostitute who tricked her father-in-law, Judah, into impregnating her, and he had to take her into his house where she delivered twin boys. Rahab ran a house of prostitution in Jericho. Bathsheba was involved in an adulterous affair with King David and maneuvered to secure the throne for her son, Solomon. And Ruth was a foreigner who traveled to Israel after her husband died, lived homeless in a pauper's field, and crept into Boaz at night asking him to marry her, a foreigner, in the very time that Ezra, the high priest of Israel, had decreed that foreign wives were condemned, and Israelite men should cut them loose to starve or go back where they came from.

What an incredible message is that family tree of Jesus. It is the greatest role reversal in history. Matthew is saying, in effect, "Whether Jesus became the Christ through a virgin like Luke's account, through a baptism by John like Mark's account or through his earthly father like my account says, is really not important. Stuff like that is not important. Look at these four women in the family tree of the son of God. Look at them. God, through Christ, has dropped the charges." There is no one that God has not dropped any charges we could bring against them. The late William Sloan Coffin often said, "There is more mercy in God than there is sin in us."

I hope that when we realize anew that Jesus has dropped the charges, we can all get our lives together and let our roles get reversed, our values get reversed, and our pessimism get reversed, especially in these times in which we live. Jesus not only loves me, this I know, but Jesus has dropped the charges for everybody I know.

Gone is the Glory?
I Don't Know

— t h e   l e s s o n s —

Now his daughter-in-law, the wife of Phinehas, was pregnant, about to give birth. When she heard the news that the ark of God was captured, and that her father-in-law and husband were dead, she bowed and gave birth; for her labor pains overwhelmed her. As she was about to die, the women attending her said to her, "Do not be afraid, for you have borne a son." But she did not answer or give heed. She named the child Ichabod, meaning, "The glory has departed from Israel," because the ark of God had been captured and because of her father-in-law and her husband. She said, "The glory has departed from Israel, for the ark of God has been captured."

–1 Samuel 4:19-22

One of the criminals who were hanged there kept deriding him and saying, "Are you not the Messiah? Save yourself and us!" But the other rebuked him, saying, "Do you not fear God, since you are under the same sentence of condemnation? And we indeed have been condemned justly, for we are getting what we deserve for our deeds, but this man has done nothing wrong." Then he said, "Jesus, remember me when you come into your kingdom." He replied, "Truly I tell you, today you will be with me in Paradise."

–Luke 23:39-43

In the ancient Hebrew language, the word Ichabod was translated "gone is the glory." As our Scripture states, the wife of Phineas named her baby Ichabod. The name was appropriate. At that time, Israel as a nation was beaten and demoralized. The symbol of God's presence among the people was a wooden box that held the covenant God made through Moses. Now that box and the covenant were in the hands of the enemy.

Gone is the glory, "Ichabod"—the name could be written across page after page of the history of many nations. The Dutch once ruled the commerce of the world—"Gone is the glory." The Phoenicians were the free enterprise champions of the ancient world. "Gone is the glory." The British created an empire that stretched around the world. "Gone is the glory."

America was once the champion of labor—a place where industry, thrift, and manufacturing reigned supreme. The holiday called Labor Day began in 1882, originating from a desire by the *Central Labor Union* to create a day off for the "working man." I laughingly told someone that I needed to write a Labor Day sermon, but it was going to be difficult because I did not speak Spanish or Chinese. Certainly, when it comes to the labor market in our country, many think "Gone is the glory."

Sometimes it would seem that we, too, are living under the sign of Ichabod. Many corporations in America have collapsed in greed. Behind every statistic of a laid-off or unemployed worker or a person who has lost his or her retirement fund lays a heap of human anxiety, desperation, and fear. "Gone is the glory."

The glory is passing from many of the old stabilities that gave certain coherence to our world. The old arrangements have broken up. We have removed most of our manufacturing to Asia where prices are cheaper. We need to do this to compete, we are told. But the arguments always compare the different costs of labor, not a comparative analysis of CEO pay. One of the biggest questions to arise in the age of globalization is how we Christians will deal with the important issues of workers' rights and forms of slavery in the developing world, and how we Christians will relate to the people who work in our own country but are not citizens.

Unregulated capitalists move their manufacturing from country to country, but there is no global government to legislate better working conditions for all. It is a challenge for Christians to address. Two thousand years ago, the Emperor of China built a wall against invaders from the north. It is still there, more or less, and it is 1,500 miles long. It stands as a great marvel of the world. It was cheap for the emperor to build, but it was most expensive for the workers. Over a million people perished in its construction.

Today, most of the people in our American society are builders and consumers. And we want to consume inexpensive goods. Sometimes we fail to tie our self-interest to the work of others. We have people around the world sweating, working, starving, and laboring in countries that are weak on human rights and safety regulations. And these people are working for us. What to do?

In a strange way, the crucifixion story, according to Luke, contains reality for you and me. You remember that Jesus was crucified among two thieves. One is there desperately afraid of the future. He starts hurling insults at Jesus: "Aren't you the Christ? Save yourself and us!"

The other thief is regretful for yesterday: "Do you not fear God . . . for we are receiving the due reward of our deeds. We are getting what we deserve, and it will get worse." Two thieves—regret for yesterday and fear for tomorrow. The author of Luke is concerned with taking the gospel to the whole world, so he attaches a lasting meaning to the conversation the thieves have with Jesus. The other two synoptic gospels just say the thieves hurled insults and leave it at that. Regardless of age, you and I are always being "crucified" between these two thieves—regret for yesterday and fear of tomorrow.

We live with yesterday's failures and successes, and we fear our tomorrows that we are unclear about. Perhaps our greatest hope lies in the fact that Jesus Christ is hanging with us right between our regret for yesterday and our fear of tomorrow.

I was in High Point, North Carolina, over two decades ago to be interviewed by a church's committee for the position of minister of the church. After the meeting was over, and I'd tried to impress them, and they had tried to impress me, one of the members came up to me. He said, "This is the third time in my life I've been on a committee to hire a minister. So far, I've been associated with one that was a success and one that was a failure."

Naturally, I asked him, "What do you consider me?"

With candor he responded, "You're I don't know."

Success, failure, and I don't know—that's the story of our lives. If you and I are to succeed as human beings, and to recover some peace of mind, it is essential that we experience some success, have some failure, and know how to live much of our lives with "I don't know." The things we can't nail down, the things we have to trust God to handle are the most challenging, aren't they?

Some of our most popular books are those that tell us how to make money and become socially agreeable. Much of our educational system is geared to a "success philosophy," preparing us for a life of banks, stocks, careers, and services. Even a great many pulpits and churches have increased their popularity by speaking mainly of how religion can be used as a tool for being a successful person, monetarily.

But somewhere between the psychiatrists helping us cope with failure and the attractive personalities on the infomercials telling us how to amass a fortune, you and I live most of our lives with uncertainty. I tell our college students, "Ten percent of your life will be a failure. You'll drop the ball, blow the assignment, anger your best friend, fail at your job, or make some screw up ten percent of the time. And ten percent of your life will be a success." You'll get the big contract, marry the pretty girl or the handsome man, catch the ball, land the big account, or make some happy acquisition; and those moments will also take up ten percent of your lifetime.

This means that at least 80 percent of your life will be spent in the realm of "I don't know how things will turn out." And this is the realm of the spirit. This is where Jesus Christ helps us the most, by being crucified and resurrected between our twin thieves of regret for yesterday's failures and fear of tomorrow's inability to keep our successes.

This, then, is the backdrop of God's amazing grace to us. When our lives are successful, God is with us. When our failures cause us remorse, God is with us to forgive. And when we face, 80 percent of our time, the uncertainty of "I don't know," there among our regret for yesterday and fear of tomorrow is a risen savior in whom we can trust. That grace is so amazing as to be one of God's greatest gifts to us.

So it was in the lives of two people, whose legacy teaches us how we are to view not only laborers but all humans. When we consider our Christian obligations to our neighbors, it is impossible to overestimate the importance of William Wilberforce and John Newton of England, and their heroic campaign to end slavery.

Wilberforce thought it peculiar that so many refined, educated, wealthy and polite members of his society could turn deaf ears to the cries of millions. Wilberforce took seriously the ideal of the world as a beloved community of which the prophets and Jesus Christ spoke. Wilberforce saw the idea that all men and women are created equal by God and are therefore sacred and each other's keepers. The ideas that one must love one's neighbor as oneself and that we must do unto others as we would have them do to us had been around for 18 centuries. But no entire society had taken those ideas to heart in the way Britain would under Wilberforce. The teachings of Jesus had been, frankly, a failure in the face of slavery.

But Wilberforce made those teachings successful. Slavery, of course, still exists around the world today. But what Wilberforce vanquished was something critically important: he vanquished the very mind-set that made slavery acceptable and allowed it to survive. The old mind-set viewed slavery and suffering and poverty as a part of "God's will." Wilberforce destroyed that way of thinking. Never again would educated people ask whether or not society had a responsibility to help the poor and suffering. We would only quibble about the details, whether to use public funds or private and how much and to whom to give the credit, the Democrats or the Republicans. Unforeseen to him, the mind-set slowly but surely would leap across the Atlantic and profoundly transform our nation.[3] Through hard won battles and difficult and tense decades, America began to abolish child labor and dangerous factory conditions, and to deal with the problems of widows and the sick. The United States became a champion of human rights.

What about now? Is the glory gone? Will it be out of sight, out of mind? Who will champion the causes of labor removed from our shores? I don't know. But I know what God can do with the years of "I don't know."

A man by the name of John Newton was a colleague of Wilberforce. He was a slave trader. As he stepped back from his life, he was tossed hither and yon, mentally by his regret for his past as a slave-trader and his fear for his future. He read a book by Thomas 'a Kempis titled *The Imitation of Christ*. This experience converted John Newton to Christianity. He became an Anglican minister. He truly regretted his past. It had been a failure. He bluntly called himself a wretch. But he was successful in being able to see the image of God. Newton became a harsh critic of slavery and fought it with his every breath. He wrote a song expressing his belief that Christ had taken away his regret over his failure and that Christ had removed his fear of tomorrow. And most importantly, he tried to express in that song his trust that Christ would be with him in his time of "I don't know."

John Newton lived 23 years of his adult life as a failure. He lived 12 years of his life as a successful Anglican clergyman. But he had to live the last 28 years of his life in a period of "I don't know." Newton died at age 82, in 1807, 26 years before Wilberforce died. The slave trade at the time was worse than it ever had been. The song he had written, "Amazing Grace," was unknown and sung by only a few people. All he could do was trust God, be converted himself, support Wilberforce, and speak out in behalf of others. That mantle of grace has now been passed to you, to me, and to our country. Will we accept it? The laborers may have left, but will our pulpits, our universities, and our people restore the glory of human rights and regain our influence in the world? Will we turn our backs to the cries of millions? I don't know. But I do know that the God of the prophets, of Jesus, and of Wilberforce and Newton can give us the courage and the grace sufficient to meet the challenge. When it comes to issues of human justice, perhaps the first step is to cease flying into our own weapons.

Flying Into Our
Own Weapons

— *the lessons* —

Then Rebekah took the best garments of her elder son Esau, which were with her in the house, and put them on her younger son Jacob; and she put the skins of the kids on his hands and on the smooth part of his neck. Then she handed the savory food, and the bread that she had prepared, to her son Jacob.

So he went in to his father, and said, "My father;" and he said, "Here I am; who are you, my son?" Jacob said to his father, "I am Esau your firstborn. I have done as you told me; now sit up and eat of my game, so that you may bless me." But Isaac said to his son, "How is it that you have found it so quickly, my son?" He answered, "Because the Lord your God granted me success."

–Genesis 27:15-20

Then the devil led him up and showed him in an instant all the kingdoms of the world. And the devil said to him, "To you I will give their glory and all this authority; for it has been given over to me, and I give it to anyone I please. If you, then, will worship me, it will all be yours." Jesus answered him, "It is written, 'Worship the Lord your God, and serve only him.'" Then the devil took him to Jerusalem and placed him on the pinnacle of the temple, saying to him, "If you are the Son of God, throw yourself down from here, for it is written, 'He will command his angels concerning you, to protect you,' and 'On their hands they will bear you up, so that you will not dash your foot against a stone.'" Jesus answered him, "It is said, 'Do not put the Lord your God to the test.'" When the devil had finished every test, he departed from him until an opportune time.

–Luke 4:5-13

One of the dominant characteristics of our time is a preoccupation with speed. Athletes are timed for their speed in the 40-yard dash. Business people live with their Blackberry and want instant access to everyone about everything. The salesperson wants to know how soon it can be shipped. As globalization experts point out, it is no longer the strong that eat the weak, but the fast that eat the slow.

One of our nation's greatest efforts in speed came with the initial breaking of the sound barrier. The autobiography of former test-pilot Chuck Yaeger provides insight into that achievement.[4] One of his accounts astounded me. It seems that some early test pilots actually shot themselves out of the sky. These inexperienced pilots would get a jet fighter up to two or three times the speed of sound. Then they would fire their weapons. The plane would travel faster than the bullets, and they would actually shoot their own wings off! I cannot imagine anything more embarrassing than flying into your own weapons, shot down by your own defense mechanisms. Yet that seems to happen frequently in our fast moving society.

God has given our human personality many weapons with which to encounter life. We possess "fight or flight" responses, administrative ability, anger, egos, temperaments, and grief and coping reactions.

These human characteristics are to be conscripted as defense mechanisms as we journey through life. But travel too fast, and we actually fly into our own defenses. Loss of peace of mind and depression itself are often caused when we out-run our brain.

For several months, I labored with the Pepsi-Cola Company in Purchase, N.Y., to get an electronic scoreboard donated to a park in High Point. Finally, the scoreboard arrived and a crew from our city installed it. It worked fine for two games, showing runs, hits, errors, the inning, and the balls, strikes, and outs. Then, rather mysteriously, during the second evening of operation, it froze. The control box would not activate it. We had to shut it down. Someone took the control box home and tested all the connections. They were fine. We thought we had big trouble. But the next day, an electrician from the city came out. Without looking at anything, he discerned the problem: "Somebody pushed all the buttons at the same time," he said. "You can't push but one or two buttons at a time. It can only handle so much current. Go beyond what it can bear, and it goes out." In like manner, our human brain can handle joy, frustration, grief, love, anger, and pretty much everything that passes through it—that is, one or two things at a time. Push all the buttons at once, and it freezes; it becomes catatonic.

The Bible tells us that right after he was baptized, Jesus Christ faced the greatest temptation of his life. He had just realized that he was the Messiah. He was at the point of beginning his ministry. Satan tempted him to try to live his whole life in a moment's time. Satan promised him instant accomplishment of his ministry. Listen to the account: "The devil led him up to a high place and showed him in an instant all the kingdoms of the world. And he said to him, 'I will give you all their authority and splendor . . . so if you worship me, it will all be yours.' " (Luke 4:5-7) Just like that, promised the devil, "You can have instant achievement. No waiting. No having to grasp the slow wisdom of the world. Here's a shortcut. Just for the taking, all can be yours in an instant."

We wonder why the Scriptures depict evil trying to trick Jesus into outrunning life. Well, the same tactic had worked countless times before. Evil has had a history of getting individuals to fly into their own weapons. It had worked with Jacob. You remember the story. Old Isaac, who has poor and failing eyesight, tells his oldest son, Esau, to bring him some tasty food and game to eat so that before he dies, he can bless Esau.

Rebekah, the mother, overhears the conversation. She tells Esau's twin brother, Jacob, and together, Rebekah and Jacob hastily prepare the old man's favorite meal. Jacob, pretending to be Esau, dresses like his older brother and brings the food to Isaac. Isaac poignantly asks, "How did you find it so quickly, my son?" Usually it takes time and a great effort and lots of work to produce this. And Jacob uses the cover up for scam and fraud that hustlers have used for centuries when he responds, "Hallelujah, the Lord gave me instant success."

Now, Jacob stole most of what would have been his anyway. By law, after the passage of time, Esau would have had to turn over a certain amount of the estate to Jacob. Jacob simply wanted it in an instant. Maybe he was lazy. Maybe he feared it would shrink in value. All Jacob's ego and assertiveness buttons were pushed by temptation at the same time. It took him decades to recover from it.

It is a strange phenomenon in life that our strengths, our weapons, can become our undoing. Many a personal and national history attests to that. Today's world is a very complicated and changed world. Our society has in this mortgage crisis been hampered by many short-sighted people who over-ran their common sense in the pursuit of individual bonuses and short-term gains without credible equity.

History seems to repeat itself. We are infatuated with the rise of China and even are somewhat dependent on China. But we could learn a lot from China's past. China was once the most scientifically and economically advanced society in the world. The Chinese began printing 600 years before Johannes Gutenberg introduced the technique to Europe through Germany. They built the first chain drive 700 years before the Europeans. They were using a magnetic compass at least 100 years before a reference to one was made anywhere else in the world. This past month, engineers from America went to the Sichuan Province to study a huge irrigation project that was created 2,300 years ago. That project was cracked by an earthquake that recently occurred, but it is still standing. When it was created, only the Mesopotamians had anywhere close to a similar system. But 700 years ago, in the middle of the 15th century, this fantastic civilization suddenly ceased their spectacular progress.

What happened to them? Why did their inventiveness dry up? Well, they became obsessed with bureaucratic rank. They grew greedy and individualistic. They ceased creating a mercantile class to foster competition and self-improvement. They lost contact with their working class; they succumbed to egoism and totalitarianism. In short, all innovation and investment in engineering and manufacturing and technology went out the window. They started competing only for rank and privilege in a culture of selfishness. They produced no idea or invention of global impact over the next five hundred years.[5] They flew into their own weapons and shot their wings off. From a culture of trust and innovation, they moved to mistrust and privilege. They over-ran their own life and haven't recovered in over 500 years. In fact, "new China," with its rote learning and one party system and government control of business, is hardly a haven for innovation.

When I was in high school, I loved to participate in the sport of track. One of the events I loved to run in was the 440 relay. This was before the days of track measurements being in meters. Each team had four men who would each run 110 yards. You carried a baton, and after your leg of the event, you passed it in full stride to the next man who would already be in motion as you approached him. One of the keys to success, of course, was to stay smooth and focused and make a clean pass so a teammate could easily receive the baton within the exchange zone.

Our relay team had three very fast boys and an average runner named Sam. The coach always puzzled over where to run Sam. If he ran the lead-off leg, the next three runners had to catch up. If we ran Sam last, the other teams would run their fastest boy at the anchor, and we never knew just how much of a lead Sam would need to keep from losing. Consequently, we would end up running Sam third. Usually, we would get Sam a large lead and if he could come even close to holding it, we would be in great shape with a fast person still to run.

On our relay team was a boy named Jeff. Jeff was the state champion in the 100 yard dash. In fact, Jeff later became the Atlantic Coast Conference champion in the 100 yard dash. He had tremendous acceleration and a tremendous will to win. Those were his greatest weapons.

We came to the regional track meet, and I just knew we had first place in the bag. I went out to the anchor spot and saw that our biggest rival was running at anchor, a boy I'd beaten by five yards in the 100 yard dash heats. If we were close to the lead, it would be a cake walk.

Well, Charlie, our lead man, took off and ran the best leg of his career. He had two yards on the field when he passed it off to Jeff. Jeff widened the lead to five yards and then to seven yards. Even Sam wouldn't lose seven yards. As Jeff rounded the curve, 20 yards from Sam, he yelled, "Go Sam, go Sam!" But Sam, ever cautious, just stood there. At 15 yards away, Jeff yelled, "Go Sam!" But Sam waited. It was okay. At ten yards away, Sam just turned around to start his trot. With about five yards to go, Jeff, whose adrenaline was really flowing and whose anger at Sam for not starting sooner was pitched, reared back, screamed, and threw the baton at Sam's head. The baton missed Sam and went sailing into the infield. I never got to run. Sam never got to run. We came in last. Jeff over-ran his resources in his will to win. Jeff wanted something in an instant that would have easily been ours in the long run anyway.

The writer of Ecclesiastes wrote that he had looked out on the world and seen the following: "The race is not to the swift, nor the battle to the strong, nor bread to the wise, or riches to the intelligent, nor favor to the skillful; but time and chance happen to them all."

We have learned some painful lessons in that regard. Democracy cannot out-run a concerned and informed citizenry. We have to invest in character as much as we invest in the stock market. We have to pause and think in the midst of the cacophony of noise about how instantly people can have their wishes come true. Often the generation that follows us asks, "How did you find what is our favorite meal so quickly?" We can't respond like Jacob of old, "Hallelujah, the Lord gave me instant success." Neither can we throw the baton over their heads in our anger and our will to win when they don't start running when we want them to run.

Some people want Christianity in quick doses, a few sound bites, and in a party atmosphere. Some want only to worship with their own age group and follow a bouncing ball of enthusiasm and praise singing. We have a very Christian society. It is not ungodly or atheistic. It's just that it has often out-run church and the teachings of the Christ who founded it. I'm not naïve enough to think we'll ever go back to those old prayer meeting days of meditation, remembering in prayer your sick neighbors, and actually thinking about theology and the meaning of life. But we need to go somewhere like that. This Jesus was on to something when he left us a church and his spirit of peace. He left us something for our souls in a world of speed. "I am the way, the truth, and the life," he said. "Put the kingdom of God first in your life, and everything else will fall into place."

We have to abide by this premise. Otherwise, we might shoot ourselves down, individually and as a culture.

Living Dog Or Dead Lion?

—— *the lessons* ——

So if anyone is in Christ, there is a new creation: everything old has passed away; see, everything has become new! All this is from God, who reconciled us to himself through Christ, and has given us the ministry of reconciliation; that is, in Christ God was reconciling the world to himself, not counting their trespasses against them, and entrusting their message of reconciliation to us. So we are ambassadors for Christ, since God is making his appeal through us; we entreat you on behalf of Christ, be reconciled to God.

–2 Corinthians 5:17-20

But whoever is joined with all the living has hope, for a living dog is better than a dead lion. The living know that they will die, but the dead know nothing; they have no reward, and even the memory of them is lost. Their love and their hate and their envy have already perished; never again will they have any share in all that happens under the sun.

–Ecclesiastes 9:4-6

M ost of us are familiar with the phrase "the bottom line." It means that no matter what happens, we, at some point, have to take a stand or explain where we are. In terms of a budget in the business world, we can spend all we wish, as long as we do not go beyond the amount budgeted, "the bottom line" for that account. There are a number of bottom lines in life that we seldom think about. But when they occur, our explanations become critical for our peace of mind.

For many of us, the sanctity of life itself is our bottom line. My long-time friend, Fred Buechner, has a quote that I have on the wall in our home. It says, "If there's anything half so much fun as being alive, I'd like to know what it is." Certainly, in *most* situations, you and I would want to stay alive instead of die. Yet that is not as simple as it might first appear.

My wife's late mother resided in an Alzheimer's special care unit the last six years of her life. When you visit that unit and others like it, you have to ask yourself some serious questions about your bottom line in life. These people do not know their children. They can't remember how to eat or dress themselves. Yet they can walk around and talk. They are like little children. One lady thinks she's at the beach. Another person, a former preacher, thinks another lady there is his wife, and they go everywhere together holding hands.

When visiting such a unit, you certainly have to have a sense of humor, or you will be overwhelmed by tragedy. You see people who were "lions" at one time. They were lawyers, physicians, mothers, fathers, preachers, and leading citizens in their communities. Now, to some people's eyes, they are more like living dogs.

As our society becomes an aged one, medical science has so improved at keeping us alive that experts say that in the near future, it is highly possible that one-third of the people in America will have Alzheimer's disease. I put that in perspective for my college students by informing them that they have a greater chance of contracting Alzheimer's disease than getting AIDS, becoming addicted to drugs, including alcohol, or having a heart attack. We have living wills; we give our children statements about a desire for a natural death; and we push for "death with dignity," as if any death could be totally *dignified*.

Death is certainly the "bottom line." It's been that way from the beginning of time. I'm amazed at the gospel versions of how people viewed Jesus. For example, the Sunday before Easter is called Palm Sunday by Christians. Many contemporary church celebrations on that day involve children in a processional waving palm branches. Yet only one gospel writer mentions that there were palms waved when Jesus entered Jerusalem. John says a great crowd came out from Jerusalem to greet Jesus because they had heard that he had raised Lazarus from the dead. Someone who could raise the dead was what they came to see. Then, as now, people wanted a great, miraculous physician. Small wonder they became a surly mob when they found out Jesus wasn't a medicine man and would himself die a human death.

It is precisely at our deepest need that an Old Testament writer aims his book called Ecclesiastes. It's a book that speaks of the necessity of caution in the midst of wild religious claims that don't recognize reality. Ecclesiastes is a needed book in the Bible because it is a counterweight to the smug assurance and simple-minded optimism found in the Psalms and Proverbs. It calls people away from wishing and daydreaming and into a genuine hope that the joy in life comes from living it.

For the writer, the bottom line is simple: "A living dog is better than a dead lion." Now, that's a view of life with which many people would not agree. Frank Boreham was pastoring a little church in New Zealand. One Sunday, there was a heavy snow, a blizzard actually, in that village. At the Sunday School hour, no teacher showed up, and only three children came. Jack rode his pony two miles through the snow; Alec came from across the road; little Myrtle, who lived next door, also came to Sunday School.[6]

The Sunday school lesson was Ecclesiastes 9:4—"A living dog is better than a dead lion." Boreham asked the three children who had braved the elements a simple question: "Do you think that's true?"

Jack, who came on his pony, said, "A living dog is better; it's better to be alive than dead any day." That persuasion would win a lot of votes among us, wouldn't it? Better to be only a dog and be alive than to be a lion and be dead. Even when life is going badly for us, surely all of us are in love with life. We all hope in Christ that your life and my life have purpose and meaning. Certainly, we have worth in God's eyes, even if other humans view us as living a dog's life by comparison.

But Alec, the little boy from across the road disagreed. He said, "Oh, I don't know about that. To be a lion is better than to be a dog, and even a dead lion was once a living lion." All of us try to ward off mediocrity. We lionize people who succeed in life, burn themselves out, advance up the ladder, and die much too young. Better to have loved and lost than never to have loved at all. Better to have had your fifteen minutes of fame than never to have had any fame at all. We remember great people and often have to live in the shadow of them. Even dead, a lion is better than a living dog, thought Alec.

He is like the person who refuses to visit the sick, the elderly, and the dying, much less go to a funeral home. "I'd rather remember her like she was," is the reasoning. Better to die a lion, having lived but a short time, than live as a dog for a long time.

Myrtle, the little girl, said: "I'd rather be some of both—a lion but alive like the dog." Well, who wouldn't? But most of the time, that is impossible. We have to make a choice: living dog or dead lion?

The writer of Ecclesiastes hits us between the eyes. Not only does he shatter the myth that goodness is always rewarded, but he tackles a very real subject. Consider the comments I and many of you have, perhaps, heard and uttered: "If I can't be the chairperson, I don't want to be on the committee." All the time, I hear young people say, "If I can't make a grade higher than a 'C,' I'm going to drop the course." Many are the people who utter, "If I can't go to a larger, more stimulating place, command a better job, or win a more exciting position, my life is worthless."

Qoheleth, the writer of Ecclesiastes, by praising a living dog, probably set the Jewish religious world on its ear. Dogs were considered to be unclean in the Bible. The Old Testament depicts dogs coming to drink the blood of Jezebel. And the New Testament isn't much better: the dogs come and lick the sores of Lazarus. Even today, we call our messes "dog eat dog," our hot days of August "the dog days of summer," and our trivial pursuits "a dog and pony show." Has the writer of Ecclesiastes lost his mind? I think not.

Since the dawn of history, the dog has bonded with humankind. Even though it has been often cursed, it remains at its owner's side with a wet nose and a wagging tail. We even refer to it as our "best friend." Don't you wish all people were half as good as their dog thinks they are?

Consider this: The Interpreter's Bible refers to 2 Corinthians, chapter 5 as "the heart of the gospel. No passage in (Paul's) letters is more important."[7] The Christian message is fully captured in this classic statement:

> For anyone united to Christ there is a new
> creation; the old order has gone . . . God has
> reconciled us to God through Christ . . . In Christ
> God was reconciling the world to God, no longer
> holding people's misdeeds against them.

The Living Bible translates the passage as God in Christ, no longer holding people's sins against them but blotting them out. Through Christ, *God loses God's memory of our sins.* In a rather weird way, Christ takes God to the Alzheimer's unit when it comes to our misdeeds. *God can't remember our bad deeds.*

My mother-in-law, in her last six years, did not know who I was. She couldn't remember. She couldn't remember the times I lost my temper and yelled at her daughter and grandchildren. She couldn't remember all the times I failed in life and the occasions when I left promises unmet and jobs undone. She could only smile when she saw me, for she knew I was supposed to be important to her.

The former preacher in the Alzheimer's unit would just stick out his hand and welcome all he saw. He couldn't remember all the people who didn't appreciate his preaching through the years and who tried to do him in every time issues arose in his churches.

The lady who thought she was at the beach always invited all the strangers to go out to the beach with her. She couldn't remember people having harmed her with their words and deeds. She had forgotten.

All property in an Alzheimer's unit has to be communal property because they'll wear each other's clothes, sleep in each other's beds, and eat each other's food. We focus on the tragedy of this survivor's disease because victims cannot remember their loved ones. It is heart-wrenching, but there is another side. Neither can the mothers remember the pain their children have caused them. The fathers can't remember the failings of their family and their friends. The first time I walked the halls, I thought, "This is hell." The last time I was there, I thought, "This might be a lot like heaven. God has forgotten our sins."

In life, good people make many mistakes and do some wrong things. We overdraw, we overreach, and we sometimes under-achieve. But cling to life. It is so precious. All the people around us may remember our failures to their dying day. But the good news is that *God forgets*. God has a memory loss when it comes to our misdeeds. A living dog *is* better than a dead lion! And that should be a measure of comfort to us in some rather tragic situations.

Being Genuine

—— *the lesson* ——

But wanting to justify himself, he asked Jesus, "Who is my neighbor?"
Jesus replied, "A man is going down from Jerusalem to Jericho, and
fell into the hands of robbers, who stripped him, beat him, and went
away, leaving him half dead. Now by chance a priest was going
down that road; and when he saw him, he passed by on the other
side. So likewise a Levite, when he came to the place and saw him,
passed by on the other side. But a Samaritan while traveling came
near him; and when he saw him, he was moved with pity. He went to
him and bandaged his wounds, having poured oil and wine on them.
Then he put him on his own animal, brought him to an inn, and
took care of him. The next day he took out two denarii, gave them to
the innkeeper, and said, 'Take care of him; and when I come back,
I will repay you whatever more you spend.' Which of these three, do
you think, was a neighbor to the man who fell into the hands of the
robbers?" He said, "The one who showed him mercy." Jesus said to
him, "Go and do likewise."

–Luke 10:29-37

S ometimes it is hard to tell what is genuine from what is only a façade. For many years, Stuart Berger was a health and diet columnist for the *New York Post*. His superb articles had a wide readership. Berger wrote marvelous columns on how to live better and longer through diet and exercise. He wrote several best-selling books. One was titled *Forever Young–Twenty Years Younger in Twenty Weeks*. People all over America went on his suggested diets and heeded his calls to exercise in futile efforts to get themselves in shape for a big wedding or a school reunion.

In 1994, Stuart Berger died. Most of his readers were shocked to find out that he died at the age of 40 and that he weighed 365 pounds at the time of his death. People realized they were trying to live up to an image that wasn't real. How do you know when someone is genuine? In a world of internet anonymity, when we talk around the globe to strangers from the isolation of our computer screens, how do we know for certain the person described at the other end is who she or he has projected to us? What does it mean to be authentic, to be real, and to be genuine?

Margery Williams, in 1922, wrote a beautiful book titled, *The Velveteen Rabbit*.[8] It has been republished many times and is the story of a little boy's nursery. The nursery is full of toy animals. One day, a new toy rabbit comes to live there. The rabbit wants to know the secret of becoming real. He asks the skin horse, who is so old his brown coat is rubbing off, how to become real.

The old horse responds, "Real isn't how you're made, Rabbit. It's a thing that happens to you. When someone loves you for a long, long time, then you become real." The Rabbit then asks, "Does it hurt?"

"Sometimes," he answers. "Generally by the time you are real, most of your hair has been loved off, and your eyes drop out and you get loose in the joints and are very, very shabby looking. But these things don't matter at all because once you are real you can't be ugly, except to people who don't understand."

Real isn't how you're made. Real isn't how old you are. It is a thing that happens to you. And the skin horse is right. It can be wearing to be loved by someone. Loving and being loved add wrinkles and white hairs to your head and can make joints grow loose.

I wonder what Jesus really looked like. The words of the old Negro Spiritual, "Ride On King Jesus," are inspiring: "Ride On King Jesus. No man can a-hinder me. King Jesus rides on a milk white horse. No man can a-hinder me. Gonna see King Jesus sitting on a throne. No man can a-hinder me."

One afternoon, I listened to those words sung by the very formal National Lutheran Choir and also by the rollicking and marvelously boisterous Wilmington Chester Mass Choir that were recorded by a Philadelphia television station 20 years ago. When we imagine King Jesus riding on before us, what image do we see?

I have always been somewhat beguiled by the attempts of various societies and cultures to conjecture what Jesus Christ must have looked like as he rode on. In the 1950's, most of the pictures of Christ available to us were held hostage by one's race—a Caucasian Jesus for white people and a black Jesus for African Americans, for example. The Jesus of both races in those days was depicted mostly as a Jesus with baby smooth skin and a glowing halo around his head. He looked like a very thin, pious 33-year-old weakling with manicured fingernails.

Then, in the 1960's, largely due to preachers' attempts to break out of being perceived as a kind of third sex, we had an accentuation on Jesus as a real man's man. The rugged carpenter came into focus. The man who could do all that walking and speaking and riding must have had real stamina. Consequently, we perceived Jesus as a tough Mel Gibson or Sylvester Stallone or Wesley Snipes look-alike, with muscles flexed and a jogger's pair of legs at best.

Then, in the 1970's and 1980's, we tried to reconcile Jesus' appearance with the fantastic sums of money pouring into the coffers of television evangelists. More than one Evangelist explained to visitors touring their opulent headquarters, when asked about the expensive paneling flown in from England or the lavish antiques decorating even more extravagant rooms, "We think Jesus, when he returns to earth, is going to return here first, and we want him to have the very best." So, we encountered a Jesus who resembled Bill Gates or Donald Trump, riding not on a gaiting horse but relaxing on a white cloud full of money for transportation. "Flow along sweet, rich King Jesus, and take us with you, please," seemed to be the hype.

Personally, I think none of those depictions are quite accurate. Jesus was not only a Messiah and a Risen Lord. Jesus was also an enormously compassionate person. He was a genuine person. He loved everyone and showered his compassion on everyone he met. Perhaps the truest statement was that of Peter: "Jesus went about doing good . . . ." (Acts 10:38). Jesus loved people and did kind things. He was killed by the people whom He tried to love the most.

Have you ever seen the hurt in a child when he or she trusts someone and that trust is betrayed? Those are the saddest eyes you'll ever see. Have you ever seen what happens to a man whose best friends abandon him in an hour of need and then try to throw him to the wolves? He becomes stooped, depressed, and wrinkled.

Consider much of the life of Jesus. Jesus healed ten lepers and only one returned to thank him. If that were me, I'd make the other nine sick again. But he didn't. He bore it. He asked his friends to stay up with him while he went off to a garden and, in great anxiety and depression, Jesus sweated drops of sweat as thick as blood. One writer wrote that sweat flowed like blood all down his face. Then, he came out and witnessed those friends sound asleep. "Could you not stay awake with me for one hour?" He asked.

I know how it feels when a student sleeps for fifty minutes in one of my classes. I just want to grab that student and throw him out of class. Well, *all of* Jesus' students fell asleep on him in the Garden of Gethsemane. In addition, one of the 12 best friends he had on this earth sold him out to his enemies for a little pouch of money. Ride on, King Jesus.

My guess is that the man who stumbled toward Calvary was prematurely gray. He must have looked more like 103 years old than 33 years old in his appearance. His face must have contained more wrinkles than a coal miner with the black lung disease, who for decades smoked four packs of cigarettes a day and worked 50 to 60 hours a week in the coal mines. His joints must have been quite loose. He probably was mentally worn out by all the sacrifices he had made and all the abandonments of friends and mental anguish that beset him in his last days. But he was the most genuine person who ever lived. He had more compassion than all of us put together. He was the most beautiful person who ever lived. *He was ugly only to those people who didn't understand.* Ride on King Jesus.

King Jesus told us a parable about how people become real. Real is not how you are made. It is something that happens to you. Jesus said a man was beaten and left half-dead. He was unconscious, and his clothes were torn off. He was simply "a certain man." There was no clue as to his status or his accent. All we know is that he was in need. A priest came by and would not get close to him. In those days, Jews believed one had to handle a dead body in a special way; otherwise you were contaminated. A life was hanging in the balance, but the priest was worried about staying clean and not getting defiled by an improper involvement.

Then, a Levite, an upper class professional priest, came by. He had the best education money could buy. It was not his nature to get involved with people beneath his status. Since the man had no clothes and couldn't speak, who could tell what rank he came from? The Levite couldn't take a chance on being seen on the Jericho road associating with just anybody. The rumors would ruin him.

Then a Samaritan came by. King Jesus said, "The Samaritan was filled with compassion." *He* was not concerned with the man's pedigree. *He* was not concerned with the man's race. *He* was not concerned with the man's religion. *He* was not concerned with what caused the man's tragedy. *He* simply had compassion. Jesus said, "*You* go and do the same." The person may never be capable of returning the favor, but you have compassion. The 10 may not thank you; your friends may abandon you; your buddies may sell you out, but *you* go and have compassion.

Our society needs to recover a sense of human compassion. Regardless of the political landscape, the cost of oil, the value of the dollar or the ups and downs of the market, if we follow Jesus, we must become real before we die. And "real" is not how we are made; it is something that happens to us when we show compassion. The hope of the world—is that enough people can become genuine to enable this earth to be a better place for those who will be born to live in it after us.

Most of us have been the recipients of a lot more compassion than we realize. There isn't enough money in the world to buy the blessings we have received. There is only one thing we can do. We can try to show everyone around us some compassion, even though they may not seem to deserve it. Most likely they will never thank us. But at least *we will be genuine.*

Is Your God Too Mean?

—— *the lessons* ——

Then a servant girl, seeing him in the firelight, stared at him and said, "This man also was with him." But he denied it, saying, "Woman, I do not know him." A little later someone else, on seeing him, said, "You are also one of them." But Peter said, "Man, I am not!" Then about an hour later still another kept insisting, "Surely this man also was with him; for he is a Galilean." But Peter said, "Man, I do not know what you are talking about!" At that moment, while he was still speaking, the cock crowed.

—Luke 22:56-60

When they had finished breakfast, Jesus said to Simon Peter, "Simon son of John, do you love me more than these?" He said to him, "Yes, Lord; you know that I love you." Jesus said to him, "Feed my lambs." A second time he said to him, "Simon son of John, do you love me?" He said to him, "Yes, Lord; you know that I love you." Jesus said to him, "Tend my sheep." He said to him a third time, "Simon son of John, do you love me?" Peter felt hurt because he said to him the third time, "Do you love me?" And he said to him, "Lord, you know everything; you know that I love you." Jesus said to him, "Feed my sheep."

—John 21:15-17

Having lived most of my life in the southern part of these United States, the fall is my favorite time of the year. After many weeks of dry, hot summer weather, the change to cooler weather is always welcomed. In my youth, I associated the fall with campfires and trips to the mountains. In a church bus or around a bonfire beside a mountain lake, we boys and girls would sing the words of a song we had learned. It started like this: "I love the mountains; I love the rolling hills, I love the flowers, I love the daffodils: I love the fireside when all the lights are low; boomdiahda, boomdiahda, boom." We would sing round after round. Somehow, around a campfire, a pretty girl's face looked more beautiful when it was illuminated by the fire. And girls tell me a handsome guy appeared more handsome in the glow of the firelight.

Fire is still associated with romance in modern advertising. There's something about a cozy fire in a fireplace that stirs the emotions. Realtors tell sellers to be sure and have a fire going in the fireplace when prospective buyers take a tour of the home.

Those who study civilization tell us that a pivotal factor in the development of the human race was the ability to control fire. When ancient humans learned how to start fires, cook over wood and charcoal and make torches, we were on our way up in the chain of existence.

Fire is an essential symbol in religious expression, not just in modern lessons and carols or Christmas Eve services, when people fill churches, raise candles skyward, and sing "Silent Night." As early as 2500 years ago, a Greek philosopher named Heraclitus spoke of the world as having begun in fire. Stoics took his lead and spoke of the vapor that emanated from this fire as the Logos, the reason, the word, which held the world together. The writer of John's gospel said this Logos, this *word*, was there as part of creation. He then went on to tell us that Jesus was the human form of that fiery vapor. As such, the stage was set for the concept of the Holy Spirit, a divine vapor that permeates the whole universe. The symbol of Pentecost, where the Holy Spirit was let loose, is a fiery flame. Christians speak of God or Christ as a "divine spark" that lies within us. "No one lights a candle and hides it under a basket," said Jesus.

The great stories of forgiveness associated with Jesus take place beside a fire. The first fireside scene in Scripture is a bad one. It reflects three major screw-ups on the part of the disciple named Peter. Jesus has been arrested. Jesus is hauled off to the house of the high priest. Peter follows at a distance. Once Jesus is taken inside the house, some of the soldiers and other onlookers build a fire in the courtyard. Peter sits down with them. As the glow from the fire illuminates Peter's face, a servant girl recognizes him. She looks closely at him and says, "This man was with him." Peter emphatically denies that he even knows Jesus. A little later as they are still sitting by the fire, another person stares at Peter and says, "Yep, I think you are one of them." Peter replies, "No way."

The group sits there another hour, warming themselves and staring into the fire.

Another person speaks up, "Surely this guy was with them. He's a Galilean." Peter replies, "I don't know what you're talking about."

Scripture says the experience left Peter so guilt ridden that he left and wept bitterly. Peter has a weight around his heart that has the power to ruin his life. Peter represents all humans who fail to deliver on their boasting. Peter is a representative figure for us - he is likable, but he is one who makes mistakes at times, just like us. He represents the guilt we feel for our imperfections and mistakes, the guilt that weighs us down, even though we don't talk about it. It keeps us from being free to live the way we want to live. It robs us of peace of mind.

Poor Peter. Three times beside a campfire he has denied even knowing the greatest person he had ever met. But wait. It's not over. Following the death and resurrection of Jesus, there is another campfire experience for Peter. The disciples have been fishing. They have had no lunch. Their nets are empty. But a stranger on the shore helps them catch fish by giving them good advice. They finally figure out that the stranger on the shore must be the Lord Jesus. They head the boat in his direction. Peter is so excited that he dives into the shallow water and starts sloshing for shore. When he gets there, he sees that Jesus has built a campfire and has fish and bread over the burning coals.

The sight of that charcoal fire would have brought back a dreadful memory for Peter. I imagine that he stopped dead in his tracks when he saw Jesus standing beside the fire with its glow illuminating his face. Jesus says nothing to Peter. The other disciples arrive, and they all have a fish fry. They recognize Jesus as he breaks the bread. This *is* the Lord. They are having communion with Jesus after his resurrection, just as he had promised.

After the meal is over, they are still sitting by the fire. Jesus turns to Peter. He asks a question, "Do you love me?" Peter says, "Yes, Lord; you know that I love you."

Jesus accepts it and says, "Then feed my lambs."

A second time and a third, Jesus asks Peter, "Do you love me?" The response is the same, "Yes Lord; I love you."

No one can miss what is happening here. Forgiveness is happening here. The past is forgotten, and life can begin again. Three times Peter had denied Jesus around a campfire. Now, following His resurrection, Jesus forgives Peter three times around a campfire.

John's gospel was the last to be written or put together. The very last image we have of the resurrected Jesus is this fireside forgiveness. That should tell us something about the nature of God. All of us are going away from this earth, just at different rates of speed. What would you like to be remembered for? What image of yourself would you like to leave behind that most clearly expresses who you were while you were living? Jesus left behind an image of himself, not as a mean God but as one who always forgives.

In his last day with his disciples, Jesus did not leave some final commandments. Nor did he give them a copy of teachings that they could use as a sacred scripture with which to hit over the head and prove wrong the people that they disagreed with. Jesus certainly did not leave principles guaranteed to make his followers healthy, wealthy, and wise.

Jesus left forgiveness. That final scene of forgiveness sets us free to forgive others for their failures. The words to us are the same as to Peter: I forgive you. You, then, feed my sheep by forgiving them.

A friend in Knoxville, Tennessee, told me about a minister who often participates on ordination councils, which question and approve candidates for ministry. This man only asks one question, and it is always the same question. He tells them to imagine that a stranger is walking down the street toward them. He asks the candidate to describe that person theologically. In three decades, the minister has found that the candidates basically give a version of only two different answers.

Some say, "That person is a sinner in need of the redemption of Jesus Christ." Others say, "Whether the person knows it or not, that person is a child of God, loved and upheld by the grace and forgiveness of God in Jesus Christ." The experienced minister said, "Technically, both answers are correct. (So, both answers pass the examination.) But it is my experience that those who give the second answer make the best ministers."[9]

I was raised in a tradition in which no service was complete without an invitation to repent and/or join the church. The invitation was sometimes what my friend Peter Gomes calls, a "referendum on the sermon, so that it was more of an intimidation instead of an invitation."[10] The preacher would even resort to telling horrible stories of people who did not know Jesus and who died suddenly in an automobile accident or a plane crash, and were destined for hell.

People are always bringing *their* tests and *their* measurements to spiritual things. Small wonder that the God we humans have created often is presented as stingy, conservative, vindictive, judgmental, and short-sighted. A great Presbyterian minister, Dr. Paul Scherer, said that we humans are always asking God to fit our little ideas and patterns and sketches of what God ought to be and how God ought to act. Essentially, many human beings worship their own God and condemn their brothers and sisters for disagreeing not with God but with them.

Frankly, *some people should just accept the fact that their God is too mean.* The last image of God that Jesus left us was not of an angry, paranoid, unforgiving, and unloving God. From the cross to the fireside meal following the resurrection, Jesus left us an image of forgiveness. That's why we Christians call the story of Jesus *good news* for everyone. That's why in our search for peace of mind, we need to look seriously at our Lord's response to us.

PART TWO

— *What We Know About God* —

What We Know About God

— *the lessons* —

"*Pray then in this way: Our Father in heaven, hallowed be your name. Your kingdom come. Your will be done, on earth as it is in heaven. Give us this day our daily bread. And forgive us our debts, as we also have forgiven our debtors. And do not bring us to the time of trial, but rescue us from the evil one. For if you forgive others their trespasses, your heavenly Father will also forgive you; but if you do not forgive others, neither will your Father forgive your trespasses.*

"*Do not store up for yourselves treasures on earth, where moth and rust consume and where thieves break in and steal; but store up for yourselves treasures in heaven, where neither moth nor rust consumes and where thieves do not break in and steal.*

–Matthew 6:9-15, 19-20

"*With what shall I come before the Lord, and bow myself before God on high? Shall I come before him with burnt offerings, with calves a year old? Will the Lord be pleased with thousands of rams, with ten thousands of rivers of oil? Shall I give my firstborn for my transgression, the fruit of my body for the sin of my soul?*" "*He has told you, O mortal, what is good; and what does the Lord require of you but to do justice, and to love kindness, and to walk humbly with your God?*"

–Micah 6:6-8

When our youngest son was in the seventh grade, he was a pretty good student. So, like many North Carolina students of that age, he got a letter from the Duke University Talent Identification Program inviting him to take the Scholastic Aptitude Test, commonly called the SAT. The College Board had a program that allowed these seventh graders to take it just for the experience. When my son returned home from taking the SAT, I asked, "How did it go?" He shrugged his shoulders and held out his hands, palms up, and gave the usual teenage response, "Fine." So I continued, "Well, did you answer many of the questions?"

He matter-of-factly replied, "Yeah, I answered *all* the questions. I guessed at most of them."

I retorted, "You weren't supposed to wildly guess. They take off more points for wrong answers than for leaving some blank. Didn't the proctors tell you that? The SAT wants to measure what you know, not what you've guessed at."

"Well," he said, "all my friends, the other seventh graders, guessed and answered all the questions, too."

For seven years, teachers had encouraged these teenagers not to leave anything blank on a test. Then, one Saturday they expected them to suddenly do an about face and leave questions unanswered on a test, if they didn't know the answer. It didn't work. The students were used to getting their grades lowered when they left a question unanswered on a test, and they weren't going to take any chances.

Most of our lives, we are taught to look like we know what we are doing, even if we don't; a guess is better than an admission that we don't know anything. We, as a society, put unlimited faith in those who act like they know what they are doing. We even have a new field in advertising and government called "Perception Management." Perception managers make up "facts" to cover the gaps in people like political candidates or religious leaders. But really, now, wouldn't we all like to see a politician stand up and say, "I know nothing about that, but I will try to learn about it so I won't be so ignorant?"

We do not come to church to do perception management for God. We are not in churches to learn how to manage the gaps in our knowledge about God, so we can get applause from the scientists, the businesspeople, and the medical professionals about how God shines in all those fields. We are here to reaffirm the treasures that are inside each of us.

These gifts of love are our treasures to share, to keep and hold within ourselves. They are not like the material things we purchase. The Scripture is correct: material gifts break. They get stolen. They decline in value. They rust. They even get lost. Consequently, we are told that where our treasure is there will be our heart, also. So let's try to name what we know about God and reaffirm it.

From our human experiences in life, from God's revelation through Scripture, and from the witnesses of those who lived and died before us, what do we know about God that we don't have to guess about? When I open my Bible and try to prepare a sermon, I often think, "How do I try to explain each week in a new way that a Jewish baby born to a peasant carpenter and his unmarried bride is our answer to many of life's questions?"

The Bible holds up the life of Jesus Christ and says there are *two things* that we can really know about God. The first is that God knows and loves all human beings, including those who believe a bit differently than we do. The other thing we can determine about God is that we know what God wants from us: to love our fellow humans on this planet and to work for their justice. "Love the Lord your God with all your heart, with all your soul, and with your entire mind, and love your neighbor as yourself," are the words quoted from the sayings of Jesus. *God is both love and justice.* If you love God, you have to take the justice part, too. If you work for justice, you have to take the loving part, also. The Scriptures and human experience are pretty clear about that.

God sees how the Egyptians are beating up on the Israelites, and God hears their cries. God comes down to deliver them. God sees how the Jews are beating up on the Samaritans. God comes down through Jesus to deliver the Samaritans from such abuse. God sees how religious leaders are taking advantage of widows, children, orphans and the poor. God comes down in Jesus to teach us how to be just and kind to one another, forgiving and helpful. God sees people ignoring the sick, the imprisoned, the hungry, and the destitute. God, through Jesus, tells us to take care of these whom society has hurt.

One day some years ago, a Catholic priest friend of mine mailed me a copy of a speech that Cardinal Keeler, Archbishop of Baltimore, gave to the National Conference of Catholic Bishops, of which he was the president. Cardinal Keeler referred to a story in the "Washington Post" that showed a shadowy side of life. It was the story of a little girl who had lost hope.

"Jessica Bradford is eleven years old," the story explained. "Jessica knows five people in her neighborhood who have been killed. It could happen to her, she says. She has known since she was in the fifth grade what she wanted to wear at her funeral. 'I think my prom dress is going to be the prettiest dress of all,' Jessica said. 'When I die, I want to be dressy for my family.'"[1]

Children who live close to carnage and death take in such things. So like Jessica, they begin planning their own funeral. The story of Jessica, age 11, already planning her funeral, was a story of lost hope.

Seven years later, I wanted to use the illustration in a sermon at the university where I preach and teach. Jessica would then have been 18 years old, if she was still alive. I wrote Cardinal Keeler, asking him to use his resources to see if he could find out if Jessica had lived. I asked him, "Does anyone know where Jessica is? Did she make it to her 18th birthday?" After a period of a few months, I received a response. They had looked hard and long, but they could not find Jessica Bradford. They did not know what had happened to her. I am sure they looked hard; the Archbishop of Baltimore had considerable resources at his disposal.

With what we know about God, we can be certain that should this girl have died, she died comforted by the arms of a loving God. Though, perhaps, orphaned by her culture, she would never, never be orphaned by her God. That much we know about our God. God has always shown a preference for the poor, the disposed, and the orphaned.

Virtually every world religion was founded by an orphan. Siddhartha Gautama, known as the Buddha, was an orphan—his mother died when he was but one year old, and he was raised by his aunt. The father of Confucius died when Confucius was only three years old. He was raised in poverty by a mother, who herself died at age 23. Moses, the founder of monotheism and the nation of Israel, was adopted by an Egyptian princess when he was three months old, given an Egyptian name, and was so orphaned from his culture that he had to use his brother, Aaron, to translate his words to his native people. The father of Mohammed died when Mohammed was six years old. He was raised by an uncle.

Jesus of Nazareth, born in an animal cave, apparently lost his father when he was twelve years old. By law, He had to take care of his widowed mother until he was 30 and could turn her over to the care of the next oldest sibling. His parables and teachings were laced with stories like the widow's mite, the widow and the unscrupulous judge, and the persistent widow.

To be honest with you, according to the nativity stories in our gospels, they were laying out the funeral clothes for Jesus the day he was born. According to Matthew, Jesus was only a day old when he was rushed to Egypt to avoid his death. According to Luke, he was eight days old when his parents took him to the temple and old Simeon laid out Jesus' funeral plans when he said, "This child is destined for the falling and the rising of many in Israel . . . and . . . will be opposed." (Luke 2:34-35)

But God took care of him, with love and justice. We know where Jesus is—with God. And we know where His Spirit is—in our hearts. And we know what God wants from us:

> God has told you, O mortal, what is good:
> and what does the Lord require of you
> but to do justice, and to love kindness,
> and to walk humbly with your God? (Micah 6:8).

We are on earth with the challenge to live by what we know about God. That is easy to say and hard to do. I think it is easier to rail against the evils in our world and try to cover them up with easy answers than to examine the resources God has given us for living life.

These are tough times for many people in our American society. And deep down, I think we all know why that is so and what has to be done. We have tried to focus on the gaps we perceived in our children's lives, wanting them to have things we did not have. We forgot the treasures we had inside us. We gave them cash instead of confidence. We gave them entitlement instead of energy and accountability. We gave them politics and public relations instead of performance and compassion. Whether the Democrats or the Republicans rule politics may not matter in the long run as much as what the rest of us do with our lives. We have to let loose what we know about God and do it in a big way.

The way to do that is to accept and live by the Lord's response to us.

The Lord's Response To Us

— the lessons —

And to the man he said, "Because you have listened to the voice of your wife, and have eaten of the tree about which I commanded you, 'You shall not eat of it,' cursed is the ground because of you; in toil you shall eat of it all the days of your life; thorns and thistles it shall bring forth for you; and you shall eat the plants of the field. By the sweat of your face you shall eat bread until you return to the ground, for out of it you were taken; you are dust, and to dust you shall return."

–Genesis 3:17-19

Then he began to speak to them in parables. "A man planted a vineyard, put a fence around it, dug a pit for the wine press, and built a watchtower; then he leased it to tenants and went to another country. When the season came, he sent a slave to the tenants to collect from them his share of the produce of the vineyard. But they seized him, and beat him, and sent him away empty-handed. And again he sent another slave to them; this one they beat over the head and insulted. Then he sent another, and that one they killed. He had still one other, a beloved son. Finally he sent him to them saying, 'They will respect my son.' But those tenants said to one another, 'This is the heir; come, let us kill him, and the inheritance will be ours.' So they seized him, killed him, and threw him out of the vineyard. What then will the owner of the vineyard do? He will come and destroy the tenants and give the vineyard to others. Have you not read this scripture: 'The stone that the builders rejected has become the cornerstone; this was the Lord's doing, and it is amazing in our eyes'?"

When they realized that he had told this parable against them, they wanted to arrest him, but they feared the crowd. So they left him and went away.

–Mark 12:1-12

When I was a teenager, my best friend's relatives would gather each fall at their family's "old home place" near Atlanta, Georgia. They frequently included me. There would be six adults and ten children crammed into one house in the country for three days and two nights. Everything, at least to my childhood eyes, always seemed to go fabulously. My friend's father was an even-tempered person who was almost always in command of his emotions.

One Sunday, as we packed to return home, it started raining. All the relatives were gathered on the back porch, watching this man pack the trunk of his car. His wife came out in the yard and stood there under her umbrella giving him instructions. For ten minutes or more, she kept up an incessant cadence: "Put this here; put that there." Finally, he had had enough. He started flinging items out of the trunk and all over the yard. He flung out all the suitcases, garment bags, travel kits, and packages. Clothes went everywhere—in the mud puddles and on the hedges. His wife just stood there crying in the rain. I can still visualize her holding that umbrella and crying while her sister was comforting her, and the rest of the relatives on the porch were laughing. One of them whispered in my ear, "He just hit his cracking point."

Even the most passive and sedate person has a cracking point. A problem begins in anger, broken relationships, immense egos, lack of communication, resentment, stress, or moving too fast until a cracking point is reached. Then, the debris is scattered all over the backyard of our horizon.

An American Medical Association survey asked several thousand general practitioners across the country, "What percentage of people that you see in a week have needs that you are qualified to treat with your medical skills?" They found that 75 percent of the people who see a general practitioner may have no medically treatable problem. Most of the physicians said they prescribed tranquilizers. The patients are ill and suffering real pain. But, essentially, a problem that begins when lifestyles and/or relationships reach a cracking point moves from one bodily system to another until it stops at some particular organ with nowhere else to go. Then the doctor can practice "end organ medicine."[2]

If we were, as the Bible contends, "created in the image of God," then God must have a "cracking point," too. There have been times, if Scripture is correct, when God has reached God's cracking point. That point seems to come when humans forget that they are tenants in this world and not owners of either the world or anyone who lives in it with them.

It started with Adam and Eve. The Lord gave them everything. God put up with everything they did. God saw that the humans were hungry and built a garden. The loneliness of mankind beat God down so God created a female companion to complete him. The dominance issues of humans gnawed at God so God let the humans name every living thing on the planet and be stewards of it. All God said was, "Don't try to become like me and take my place. Enjoy everything, but don't try to take over the knowledge of good and evil."

A tempting force came along and said, "God won't crack. Don't worry about it. You can do anything. You can have your eyes opened and be like God." Sounds like a motivational speech: "God wants you to step up and grab it all. No limits, no accountability; you can do this."

So they tried it. At the time of their greatest success, Adam and Eve ran into God's cracking point. Like the man hurling baggage from the trunk of a car, God called out the debris God was going to leave all over the backyard of humankind. "I will greatly multiply your pain in childbirth; you will have to earn a living all the rest of the days of your life; you will sweat and toil; and when that's over, you will return to the ground from which you were taken; you are dust and to dust you shall return." (Genesis 3:16-19) Then God drove them out of the garden. Human arrogance *is* God's cracking point.

The last parable Jesus ever told points to God's cracking point (Mark 12:1-12). The parable of the wicked tenants pictures God dealing with humans who resent the fact that they are only renters. A man plants a vineyard, digs a pit for a wine press, rents it out to tenants, and leaves. When harvest time arrives, this owner sends a servant to get some fruit from the tenants. They beat him up and run him off. Twice more the owner sends servants. They beat one of them up and kill the other one. All the owner has left is a beloved son. So he sends him, saying, "They will respect my son." But the renters have become profiteers. They want to steal the property. They are elated when the son comes. They kill the heir and get all the money.

Jesus responds, "What will the owner do? He will come and destroy the tenants." When the scribes and priests heard this, they exclaimed, "God forbid!" The meaning is clear—*woe be unto us if we try to give ourselves the things that God owns and if we abuse other workers in the process.* That's God's cracking point. When we use other people to selfishly maintain our egos or our own high standard of living, God cracks up. When our own ambition wildly leads us to covet things that are not ours, God cracks up. When we sever relationships with other people and jealously try to use and steal for our self promotion the dignity of other people, God cracks up.

Fortunately, humans and God have in common more than
an ability to reach a cracking point and shout into the rain, "I just
can't take it anymore." In fact, how we respond to life beyond the
cracking point is extremely important. And we can look to God
for an example of how to do that, as well. *When you get on the other
side of your cracking up point, that's when you have to return to your essential understanding of love.* Remember the end of story of the fall of
humankind in the Garden of Eden?

The humans have pushed the limits. They have blown paradise.
But God responds with love and care. God makes them clothes
since their innocence is gone. God does not divorce them from each
other but keeps them together as a couple. God can no longer give
them protection from the harsh realities of the world, but God gives
them God's presence. God goes with them outside the Garden.
God gives up paradise also. God forgets the broken relationship
and tosses it overboard, so to speak. That's God's response to the
situation. It's called unconditional love.

One spring day in Washington, D.C., an excursion boat was
on the Potomac River on its maiden run. A large number of con-
gressmen and senators were invited. The day was a hot one. So a
famous senator removed his shoes and socks. He hung the socks on
a railing in front of him. One of the members of the press noticed
that someone ran by him and inadvertently brushed against one of
the socks. It fell into the water and was gone. The Senator went over
to the railing, picked up the remaining sock and threw it overboard.
The columnist was impressed. He confessed that if it had been him,
he probably would have brought the remaining sock home. "I have a
. . . drawer full of single socks . . . " he said. "That's my problem. My
life is full of single socks. I've got to clean out these good-for-nothing
things and get down to some new simple responses that work."[3] In
like manner, I once saw a woman at a picnic take her husband's
Blackberry from the table after he had texted his way through the
meal. She threw it into a lake. She said she was tired of half conver-

sations, half attention spans, and total disregard for people.

Sometimes things need to be jettisoned so we can return to a new appreciation of how we should respond to people. We should remember what God did in Jesus to respond to the wicked tenants of God's vincyard.

A great dramatization of God's response to humankind was given by a man from Greensboro, North Carolina, named Marc Connelly. In 1929, Connelly, a black man, wrote a play called The Green Pastures.[4] It was an attempt to portray in the language of the Deep South a vision of God and God's heaven. In Connelly's view of heaven, the angels hold some magnificent fish fries. The final scene revolves around just such a fish fry. A large kettle of hot fat has a fire going underneath it. A rustic table is piled high with piles of biscuits and cornbread, and the cooked fish are in huge dishpans. There are two large churns of custard, which looks like milk. The angels are milling around, flapping their wings. But God is seated in an armchair with his face in his hands. Every now and then he looks up and stares out toward earth and cries. The angel Gabriel walks in and comes up to the armchair.[5]

"You look worried, Lord," Gabriel says. God nods his head. "Here, have a cigar, Lord." But God says, "No thanks, Gabriel; don't want any cigar." Gabriel goes over and gets a cup of custard. Then he returns. "You look awful, Lord. You've been sitting here looking this way an awfully long time. Is it something serious, Lord?" God responds: "Very serious, Gabriel. Look at my children down there on earth. They are killing one another. Stealing from and lying to each other. They are running after money and status and feeding their egos at the expense of others. My heart's broken."

Gabriel is awed by his tone. He knows the Lord just can't take it anymore. "Lord, has the time come for me to blow the horn? Just say the word, Lord. Just snap your finger, and I'll blow the horn. We'll wipe 'em all out dead right now. Say the word, Lord, and I'll blow the horn."

God waves Gabriel off. "Not yet, Gabriel; I've decided what I'm going to do. I'm going to go down there myself. I'm going to live among 'em. Eat among 'em. Love 'em. Help 'em. Even die among 'em if I have to." The Lord gets up from his armchair and walks away from the fish fry. Gabriel goes over to the empty chair, and he stares down at earth. All the heavenly beings come over and look down, too. And from the back, a voice is heard: "Oh look at him! Look at him. They are going to make him carry that cross up that high hill! They are going to nail him to it! They are going to nail him to it! Oh, that's a terrible burden . . ." But as the light fades, they see the Lord down there smiling gently. And all the angels burst into song. *Because they'd seen how the Lord responded to us after he got to his cracking point.*

The story in Genesis is not about the garden. It is about the humans and how God responds to them after God has reached the cracking point. The parable Jesus tells about the vineyard comes before his death on the cross. The love of God has the last say in both incidences.

It does not take a genius to realize that we have some problems in our society at this time in its history. From corporations, to families, to universities, to churches, we have the price tags all messed up in many aspects of life. We have not been treating people as well as we can. Gaps have been created economically and personally—egoism and selfishness have run amuck. We could be at a cracking point.

The Lord has shown us how to respond. We respond to others the way the Lord has responded to us. Unconditional love is the only way out of any mess. Whether the mess is in a family or in a corporation or in a university or in a society, unconditional love for everyone in the sphere of influence is the only lasting way out. And because the Lord God lives, we can believe in the eternity of the love that God has given to us, even in the midst of some of the stupid things we humans choose to do.

Forgiveness Of Stupidity

—— *t h e   l e s s o n s* ——

Then Jesus said, "Father, forgive them; for they do not know what they are doing." And they cast lots to divide his clothing.

–Luke 23:34

Everyone then who hears these words of mine and acts on them will be like a wise man who built his house on rock.

–Matthew 7:24

F or my birthday one year, my wife Diane, at the encouragement of our two sons, gave me an iPod. My children, perhaps correctly, viewed me as a dinosaur for not having had one. They were embarrassed that I used a Walkman with big earphones that looked like something Forrest Gump wore while running around the country in the movie by the same name.

My oldest son worked with my electronically challenged brain to get over a hundred "old school" beach music and country music songs loaded onto the iPod and proceeded to develop my play lists. He showed me how to push the middle button to cut on the iPod and how to hold another spot to cut it off. Then he left and went back to his own home. It was great to listen to the contraption as I worked out three mornings a week at the fitness center in High Point. But I encountered a big problem. The thing kept cutting back on every time I touched it, put it in my pocket or gym bag, or laid it down. Consequently, the battery kept running down. I was recharging it every few days. Finally, I would put it on the passenger seat of the car where I knew nothing could touch it, or bump it and accidentally cut it on.

One day, the iPod came back on in my pocket just from bouncing against my body when I sat down. I decided that maybe

I did not want an iPod. In fact, I couldn't see why anybody would want one. I called my daughter-in-law to see if hers worked any better than mine.

She told me over the phone that there is this little button right on top. You push the button to the side and it locks the iPod to keep it from coming on. I was stupid for not taking the time to ask the right questions or read the directions.

We all are ignorant and stupid about different things. Some are not important, but some can become tragic.

A couple that Diane and I know and love very much lost a grandchild. The young man was only 19 years old. He and three friends went drinking and racing on a two lane road just outside the city limits. The car flew into the air and all were killed. The grandfather, reflecting on the incident, sadly remarked, "He was not a bad kid. But he did some stupid things. Sometimes good people do stupid things."

The entire human race, in fact, has often been hampered as much by its stupidity or its foolishness as by its sinful behavior. Wisdom has nothing to do with education. Educated people can be quite stupid in some ways, and many often are. On the other hand, people with little formal education can be very wise.

My father was a very wise person. He never finished the sixth grade. But he was wise. The last time I saw him alive, he was in his hospital bed, curled into the fetal position in pain from the cancer that was claiming his life. As my oldest son and I sat there, he said, "I don't think I'm going to be with you much longer. Always remember to be honest, and realize that many of the things you possess came to you because you were lucky enough to be surrounded by great people and live in great places, not because you were necessarily better than other people."

I was amazed at his wisdom. Many of the things I viewed as personal achievements, he viewed as gifts to me from others.

On the other hand, the smartest and most educated person

I ever taught was perhaps one of the most stupid. This person graduated from Johns Hopkins University with a 4.0 average. She had a 4.0 in graduate school at an Ivy League institution. But no company would hire her. She was the most arrogant, discourteous and ungrateful person most people ever met. She finally had to take a job in a foreign country, the Philippines. No one, literally, in the United States would hire her.

So hampered have we human beings been by our own stupidity that Marc Connelly tried to capture it in the play *Green Pastures*. With a Southern drawl, the angel Gabriel comes to "de Lawd" in a panic and says, "Gawd, your chillen are at it again, they are fighting and feuding and killing each other." The Lawd asked, "Which chillen, Gabe?" He responds, "You know, Lawd, dem stupid ones you put down on earth." Indeed, God's earthlings seem to have always had problems expanding their beliefs to include other people.

Morality in a mathematical definition is this: the fewer persons we are concerned about as we consider what to do with our power, the less moral an action is; the more people we take into consideration as we consider the impact of our actions, the more moral it becomes. In business, there has to be a balance between shareholders and stakeholders. Good business can only operate in an environment where people have long-term balance between running up quick short-term profits and considering the long-term well being of the whole group of people who are affected by its decisions.

Jesus, himself, taught that the more people we take into consideration as we consider our lifestyle, the more Godly we become. The Jews hated the Samaritans, so He told a parable in which a *Good* Samaritan was the hero. When he encountered people who hated the Romans, He found a Roman who was living an outstanding life and said, "Not even in Israel have I found such faith as this Roman has." The people in Jesus' nation hated the Sidonians, their neighbors. Consequently, Jesus climbed up into the pulpit and preached about Elijah being sent to the land of Sidon to a woman who was a widow.

Whoever and wherever Jesus encountered stupidity, He matched it positively with something far better.

The teaching familiar to us has been that Jesus was crucified by *sin* to overcome the *sin* of the world. Actually, He seems to have been crucified by the *stupidity* of the world to overcome the *stupidity* of the world. Indeed, it was a crazy spectacle. Here was the crowd, the quintessence of 4000 years of Jewish faith from Abraham down to Joseph, shouting for the release of Barabbas, a common criminal, and demanding the crucifixion of the only completely good person they ever encountered. "Which one shall I release?" cried the Roman official. "Give us the criminal, give us the criminal," they shouted. Has ever a more stupid decision been recorded in the annals of human history?

Jesus often talked about our human tendencies. He told a parable about a stupid man who built his house on sand and a wise man who built his house on stone. There is no sin in building a house or a life on a foundation of sand. No sin at all! But it is rather stupid. He articulated that the pious, Bible-thumping Pharisees were fools because they cleaned the outside of the cup first and left the middle of it nasty. They concentrated on outward appearance rather than inward character. Jesus talked about the blind leading the blind, fool leading fool, stupid person arm-in-arm with another stupid person, until both fell in the ditch. He spoke of blind guides and ignorant professors. He told a parable of ten virgins who took their lamps to a wedding to wait on the bridegroom. Five were wise, He said, and prepared their lamps with oil in case the groom was late. Five were stupid and carried no oil. No sin, just a lot of stupidity. He told a rich young ruler, "You are a man of inward strength, but you are also a fool. You live only for appearances. You are stupid."

If the life of Christ recognized anything, it was the need to do something about the force of ignorance, especially ignorance on the part of good folk with good intentions. That's what makes the cross such an earth-shaking event. It forgives not only our sins, but our stupidity as well.

As His life's blood drained from His body, Jesus the Christ uttered the plaintive cry, "Father, forgive them; for they know not what they do; they're stupid." Is there anything as sweet as knowing that God forgives you and me for our stupid actions as well as our sinful actions? What great news—forgiveness of stupidity. If God does not forgive stupidity, many of us are doomed.

I seriously doubt that there are many people that I know who will commit maliciously intended major sins this year. Hopefully, no one reading this book will break the Biblical commandments against killing, stealing, and adultery. Yet, many, myself included, will do some stupid things. Isn't it wonderful to know that God forgives us for stupidity? From the lowly prostitute to the haughty tax collector, Jesus time and again said, "I forgive you; learn from it, and don't do it again." But He went on to say in effect, "Since God forgives you of your stupidity, then when people do something foolish to you, please forgive them for not knowing, for not thinking, and for not taking more into consideration before *they* acted stupidly on you."

These are precarious times in our nation. Our whole economic system has done some very stupid things. Greed, deception, and abandonment of moral and religious values have built some houses on sand in our capitalistic system. Greed, deception, individualism and short-term goals are, frankly, quite stupid. But I have hope for the future, and I don't think it is misguided.

On an episode of the old television show "Andy Griffith," Otis, the town drunk, rides into Mayberry slightly inebriated. He thinks the cow he is riding on is a horse. So Barney and Andy arrest him. They put him in the cell, which is like a second home to him. Now, Barney has received a book on psychology through the "Learn-A-Month Club." He is determined to bring treatment to Otis. In the book is a page on which there is a huge ink blob. Barney asks, "Otis, tell me what you see." Otis replies, "It looks like a bat to me." With disgust, Barney shouts, "That's the trouble with you, Otis! You see a bat, but I see a butterfly." Barney and Otis start yelling at each other, "Bat–Butterfly." "Bat–Butterfly," sort of like the Democrats and Republicans on the cable channels as they try to spin the latest three second sound bite from the mouth of their political opponents. "Bat-Butterfly."

Many Americans are finding that the economic horse they thought they were riding on is really a cow at present. They have awakened to sobriety in our consumer-oriented society and found that not only is the customer not always right, but sometimes the customer is a moron. Yet, we can still see some butterflies in the midst of human stupidity. If God can forgive the stupid, uninformed people who killed Jesus, God can surely forgive our stupid acts as well. Maybe in the process, we will also forgive others of their stupidity, work toward the public good, and replace talk of, "I want," "I need," and "I choose," with "I should," "I ought," and "I promise."

Where we have come from may not be half as important as where we could be heading—toward matching where we have been with something far more positive on the other side—a house built on a firmer foundation than shifting sand. For Christians, the forgiveness uttered from the cross on which Jesus died is not a bad place to begin any recovery.

Lifting Up A Cross

— *the lessons* —

When I came to you, brothers and sisters, I did not come proclaiming the mystery of God to you in lofty words or wisdom. For I decided to know nothing among you except Jesus Christ and him crucified. And I came to you in weakness and in fear and in much trembling. My speech and my proclamation were not with plausible words of wisdom, but with a demonstration of the Spirit and of power, so that your faith might rest not on human wisdom but on the power of God.

–1 Corinthians 2:1-5

Then Paul stood in front of the Areopagus and said, "Athenians, I see how extremely religious you are in every way. For as I went through the city and looked carefully at the objects of your worship, I found among them an altar with the inscription, 'To an unknown god.' What therefore you worship as unknown, this I proclaim to you. The God who made the world and everything in it, he who is Lord of heaven and earth, does not live in shrines made by human hands.

Since we are God's offspring, we ought not to think that the deity is like gold, or silver, or stone, an image formed by the art and imagination of mortals. While God has overlooked the times of human ignorance, now he commands all people everywhere to repent, because he has fixed a day on which he will have the world judged in righteousness by a man whom he has appointed, and of this he has given assurance to all by raising him from the dead."

When they heard of the resurrection of the dead, some scoffed; but others said, "We will hear you again about this." At that point Paul left them. But some of them joined him and became believers, including Dionysius the Arepagite and a woman named Damaris, and others with them.

–Acts 17:22-24; 29-34

D o you like giving a speech? Most people do not. Psychologists tell us that fear of having to make a speech ranks behind only fear of illness and fear of death as producing the greatest anxiety. There's nothing more humiliating than standing before a group of people and having your joke fall flat, your main point fail to get across, or your punch line fail to be appreciated.

I have a friend who is the son of a coal miner and who grew up in a coal camp. Every other year, the coal mining town where he grew up, Derby, Virginia, holds a reunion. At these reunions, my friend is the Master of Ceremonies. One year, he needed a good joke to break the ice with the audience. I told a joke one day at lunch about a golfer doing something unusual on the golf course. "That's what I need," chuckled my friend. He wrote down the entire joke on a couple of napkins for his upcoming reunion.

That weekend at his reunion, he started his speech with the golf joke. He paused. There was stone cold silence. No one laughed. He tapped the microphone to make sure it had been working. The joke was a bust. Few of those coal miners and their children had grown up with country clubs and golf courses. The illustration certainly had failed to connect with the audience.

Any minister who preaches on a regular basis has experienced a sermon that fails to connect with the audience. A significant sermon that failed to get its point across was one given by Paul in Athens. Paul never mentioned the cross of Christ, which should have been his focal point. Paul missed a great opportunity. He got caught up in the importance of the people he was speaking to. He started philosophizing. He tried to be wise. The sermon depicted in Acts 17 most likely almost put the audience to sleep. Paul droned on about an unknown God. He started waxing eloquently about humans being God's offspring. It was polished. It was wise. It was logical. It was inclusive. It was eloquent. It even quoted a poet everyone in the audience respected. It had terms like, "for in him we live and move and have our being." Some of the learned people there said, "We want to hear you again on this subject." It was like a lecture. *It did not mention the cross.* Paul made very few converts so he left Athens and went to Corinth.

Paul later admitted that his sermon in Athens had failed. He said to the Corinthians, "When I came to *you*, I did not come with eloquence or wisdom. For I resolved to know nothing while I was with you except Jesus Christ and Him crucified."

From Paul, I take it that we Christians are people who should speak about the cross. Yet the cross is a subject that demands much thought in our modern world. Some voices claim that we should do away with the cross as a symbol and cease preaching about it altogether. Many contemporary worship services view the worshipper as a customer and don't have crosses because they want everybody to feel positive and lifted up when they leave church.

You look hard in vain to find a cross in some of the megachurches. Their pastor is usually an attractive man, woman, or a married couple standing in front of a revolving globe or an empty stage and preaching a shallow message about self-actualization. The message is usually a blend of pop psychology and hero worship. They don't want the customers to experience anything negative, especially a cross.

Others don't want a cross because they have seen it misused by people. From the emperor Constantine and the Crusaders to the Ku Klux Klan to politicians, righteous indignation has killed people in the name of Christ. Killing in the name of God has saturated every fundamentalist call to arms in every religion.

Sometimes the cross *has been used* to demand self-sacrifice and suffering from the weak and sanctify abuse by the powerful. These claims deserve our attention. Any use of the term "cross" today needs a contextual basis.

We Christians have no choice but to preach the cross. *Without the undergirding of the cross, a sermon can become merely advice for self improvement, a marketing ploy for getting people to give money, or an angry diatribe against our perceived enemies.*

A theology of the cross is critical today. *It is the only symbol we have that opposes the "prosperity gospel"* present in Western economics and cultural philosophies that support individual greed, despite mass human need. Consequently, a theology of the cross may encourage Christians to see reality through the eyes of the suffering and be able to address the world's needs as did Jesus, through belief in a loving and forgiving God. The cross reveals God's love for all humankind. People often claim that they have God on their side in a war. Yet, I truly believe that God is on the side of the innocent victims, those who suffer, not those who inflict suffering.

The cross not only affirms God becoming flesh and living among us, but it also affirms God dying as we die and coming out on the other side in total victory. When one preaches the love and forgiveness of God, lives get changed at any age. Paul did learn to preach the cross, and he helped transform a little Jewish sect into a faith for the whole world. Martin Luther preached the cross and started the Protestant Reformation. Martin Luther King, Jr., preached the cross and nonviolence and transformed social and political life in America. You and I hope someone can preach the cross to us and transform the way we feel about death, since the

death ratio, in spite of modern medicine, is still one out of one.
There are a lot of people hurting in our world—there are a lot of illnesses we haven't cured.

Most Christians walk into churches that have a cross on the top of a steeple. Most sermons are delivered in front of a cross. Every proclamation is shaped by the awareness that a God of love and forgiveness always triumphs—always has the last word. Hatred, violence, and illness, as we know, have no problems in announcing themselves to the world. Love, too, must announce its intentions to the world. If the churches do not do it, then who will?

The cross was used by the ancient Romans to put an end to political uprisings. They discovered that not only is a cross a slow and painful death, but it is also public. It would serve as a deterrent to others. If you had a problem with a group, a cross out on a highway would make them scatter. It would put an end to this God business.

It appeared to work. The empty tomb of Jesus didn't make much difference to either the Romans or the disciples. Empty tombs were not that uncommon in those days. People were always stealing bodies. They said that happened to Jesus' body. Somebody obviously stole it. An empty tomb did not necessarily proclaim Jesus as resurrected. But the cross did. The cross came back as a strategy for building a new world.

Christians began to live and die as Jesus had lived and died. People began to love as Jesus had loved, and forgive as Jesus had forgiven, even when their lives were going downhill in terms of their health and resources. The cross came back in the lives of Jesus' followers, and it changed everything. Suddenly, people were scratching it on coins over the faces of the Roman emperors. People were painting crosses on walls of their homes and in caves. People were going to their deaths in the coliseum in Rome and making the sign of the cross and forgiving those who had done them harm.

Donald Caskie was minister of Scots Kirk in Paris at the time of the German invasion of France in 1940. Although he had opportunities to flee, Caskie stayed there to develop safe houses and escape routes for allied military personnel trapped in occupied territory. After aiding thousands of servicemen to freedom, he was arrested and sentenced to death. One day, he and another prisoner were taken from their cells and placed in the back seat of a car driven by the Gestapo. The other man, frail and thin, said, "They have told me I shall die today."

Caskie also was distraught. He listened to the other man speak of his young children. When the car stopped, the man tried to leave ahead of Caskie, but the Germans stopped him. They said, "The pastor gets out here; you stay in the car, for you are going to a place where you will be shot." The pastor looked at the trembling body and the pale face of the man remaining in the car and asked the guards if he could say good-bye to him. They said he could have two minutes. Caskie put his hands on his shoulders and told the man that soon the Allies would arrive and though he was to die, his children would be protected. He told him to remember the One who died on the cross for love of him and his children. "He is with you now, my friend," said the pastor "He has sent me to tell you this You die in his company. You are secure in his care and you must pray for all of us who remain."[6]

What is it that makes a church what it is? Is it the music? Is it the worship? Is it the people? These are important. But I think there is something more at work. Churches bear witness to God's power to lift up people from their crosses and redeem them at any age, regardless of their mistakes and in spite of their weaknesses, illnesses, and lack of understanding. It is the love of God as experienced on the cross that gives us peace and hope in our lives in a world that badly needs some peace and hope.

The Miracle Of Sharing

— *the lessons* —

*The day was drawing to a close, and the twelve came to him and
said, "Send the crowd away, so that they may go into the surrounding
villages and countryside, to lodge and get provisions; for we are here in
a deserted place." But he said to them, "You give them something to
eat." They said, "We have no more than five loaves and two fish—unless
we are to go and buy food for all these people." For there were about
five thousand men. And he said to his disciples, "Make them sit down
in groups of about fifty each." They did so and made them all sit down.
And taking the five loaves and the two fish, he looked up to heaven, and
blessed and broke them, and gave them to the disciples to set before the
crowd. And all ate and were filled. What was left over was gathered
up, twelve baskets of broken pieces.*

—Luke 9:12-17

*And becoming aware of it, Jesus said to them, "Why are you talking
about having no bread? Do you still not perceive or understand? Are
your hearts hardened? Do you have eyes, and fail to see? Do you have
ears, and fail to hear? And do you not remember? When I broke the five
loaves for the five thousand, how many baskets full of broken pieces
did you collect? They said to him, "Twelve." And the seven for the four
thousand, how many baskets full of broken pieces did you collect?"
And they said to him, "Seven." Then he said to them, "Do you not
yet understand?"*

—Mark 8:17-21

A reporter once interviewed the famous black singer, Marion Anderson. He asked her what had been the greatest moment in all her illustrious life. Now, Marion Anderson had enjoyed many great moments up to that point. One evening, the legendary musical conductor Arturo Toscanini had said hers was the finest voice of the century. She had given a private concert for the King and Queen of England. And one Easter, from the steps of the Lincoln Memorial, she had sung before Congress and a crowd of 75,000 people in Washington, D.C.

She certainly possessed a lengthy resume of impressive achievements. However, she did not choose one of those moments as her greatest. She was honest with the reporter. She told him that the greatest moment of her life was the day she went home and told her mother, "You don't have to take in other people's washing anymore! I've now got enough money to feed and clothe you."[7]

There is a deep satisfaction in reaching a significant personal goal. There is a much *deeper* satisfaction in being able to share the benefits of your accomplishment with someone in need of what you possess.

Trying to explain a meaningful church experience to people who have not experienced one is not an easy task. In their best sense, churches are where people whom God has blessed with abundant resources come to worship and share with each other. Many of the people own more things than the average American owns. Quite a few among worshippers in churches own more than even some ancient kings and queens owned. Yet, they come and love a place that has no great financial return on investment, revolves around lay people, and sometimes has to chill to the bone certain feelings of being comfortable with one's prejudices. How can you explain that?

Church should be a place where people are thrown back on their faith rather than their fancies. It is a place to intensely feel that regardless of your health, your station, or your age, you have something good to share with each person in the room; and they in turn have something good to share with you, if only for a morning. We are not used to that kind of sharing.

In the Middle Ages, people were *expected* to share with one another. All universities were church-related. Consequently, all professions—law, medicine, ministry, and education—carried with them an oath. That's why they were called "professions." One had to "profess" a calling to serve God and humankind above self in order to earn the honor of wearing academic regalia.

The candidates for graduation would come forward in their robes. Then each would walk up to the platform, raise the right hand, and swear an oath to serve God and humankind. A hood would then be placed around their neck and they were "graduated."

Each hood, like those of today, had a deep pouch sewn into it. In that earlier society, a doctor would wear the robe and hood to work. After treating a patient for an ailment, the doctor would stand by the exit, turning his back. The patient would drop into the hood the number of coins he or she felt the doctor's service was worth or the number of coins he or she could afford. At the end of the day, the doctor would empty the hood onto a table, and that was the doctor's salary.

In like manner, the lawyer wore the gown and hood to the

law office or the courtroom. He stood by the door when the work, from drawing up a will to arguing a case, was completed. The coins voluntarily dropped in the pouch of the hood constituted the lawyer's income.

The minister would stand by the cathedral exit, his back to the parishioners, and into the hood would go the coins from the constituency. That's how pay was obtained for a funeral or a baptism or a wedding ceremony. If we tried that today, we would most likely go broke in a hurry!

The ancient hood was one of the most honored and trusted symbols in Christendom. It meant service above self. The hood played an essential role in Jesus' greatest miracle about the Kingdom of God. Since childhood, I had labored, with alternating degrees of clarity and confusion, to understand the miracle of the feeding of the crowd. Jesus of Nazareth was confronted with a situation in which, on the surface, the sheer human need appeared far greater than available resources. A great crowd of over 5,000 people had followed Jesus. He had compassion on them. He spent all day healing and teaching them. This was no one hour worship service. This event started in the morning and lasted all day. When it was finally over, the disciples asked Jesus to send the crowds away, into the villages to buy food.

Jesus replied, "They don't have to go away. You feed them."

This dumbfounded the disciples. They thought the Lord had lost His mind and was a candidate for a remedial mathematics class. "We've only got a few loaves of bread and a couple of fish."

Jesus ordered the crowd to sit down on the grass in groups of fifty. He then called upon the disciples to give up *their food*. They gave it to Him. He held it up, blessed it, and gave it back to them for distribution. Scripture says, "All five thousand, ate and were satisfied." And 12 baskets-full of food were left over.

The miracle of sharing is understandable. The typical person in Jesus' day traveled on foot. Even the most routine visits took hours to complete. Consequently, it was customary for a traveler to carry a quantity of food hidden on his or her body. This reserve food supply was something a person traveling in the Holy Land would not be caught without. Food was an expensive commodity and was preferred over coins in bartering arrangements. Usually, the supply of food was kept in the pouch of a hood slung around your body and concealed from view by the heavy robes or tunics worn in that period of history. You didn't want to have all your valuable food out in view so potential robbers and thieves could see how rich you were. To leave home without the pouch in your hidden hood, crammed full of food, would be the contemporary equivalent of driving off on a long trip with no credit cards or cash.

For example, in the parable of the Good Samaritan, the traveler along the Jericho road was first *stripped* and then robbed and finally beaten. You had to first *strip* someone in order to rob them. Read that parable: first they stripped him of his clothes. Then when they saw how much money and food he had, they robbed him and beat him and left him for dead.

On the day of the feeding miracle, many travelers had expectantly followed Jesus. But they were surprisingly joined by many local townspeople. The townies were mixed in among the long distance travelers. These people, who lived nearby, had no food. They had expected to stay only a few hours. But the event dragged on all day. "Send them home," counseled the disciples. "No, you give them something to eat," replied Jesus.

When Jesus and his disciples were willing to take *all they had* and share it with total strangers, it produced a miracle. Can't you envision these travelers on the hillside reaching under their robes and taking out their hoods containing pouches of food they had hidden for themselves and sharing food with the townies?

By the time the travelers in their robes had gotten out in the open their hoarded resources, enough was gathered for everyone to be satisfied! Being placed in face-to-face relationships in little groups of fifty persons each turned the "crowd" into dealing with individuals.

Remember now, this was a miracle about the nature of the Kingdom of God. Jesus flatly stated, "You can do even greater miracles than I have done." We must remember that all Jesus' religious stories were meant to have a real world effect. As Mark's gospel clearly notes, the disciples could not quite get it. Jesus kept asking them, why don't you get it? "You have ears but do not hear and eyes but do not see!"

The essence of the miracle is not in its display of power, nor in its ability to attract attention and high visibility, but in its capacity to meet and satisfy human needs. The feeding of the crowd was not the miracle. The miracle was that in the sharing of their hoarded possessions, the people had their eyes opened. They saw Jesus and his sharing with strangers as God's message to the world.

We gather in churches, whatever our age, in a journey through a culture that is desperately trying to ward off all kinds of social disasters. We encounter neighborhoods that are becoming more impersonal, with people drawn to drugs, crime and violence, racial and gender stereotypes, and political demagoguery. We have earned tons of trinkets in this morally confused world.

Hark, hark, the dogs do bark.
The beggars are coming to town.

Some in rags and some in tags,
and some in velvet covered gowns.

What are we velvet-covered beggars to do? Right now, we can embrace the miracle of sharing that takes place among those who know what God wants. When we are willing to take what we have, sing our songs together, open our hearts to the mystery of God, and think high thoughts with people who worship with us because they also want to think high thoughts, we become as a group, something far better than we are as individuals in whatever city or state we worship. There will be baskets full of satisfaction left over.

We embrace the majestic presence of God in old and rugged places as well as in new and smooth places. As we sit together, the past speaks to us. And the future seems less frightening because we can discern the permanent in that which is dying. In a genuine way, our eternal life will have begun on earth as it will be in heaven. In heaven, there is nothing but sharing. The miracle is always in the sharing of who we are and what we have with one another on our march toward the distant voice that calls us home as faithful servants of God. We begin to experience an upward pull that may be our strongest asset as we try to process what we know about God.

The Upward Pull

—— *the lessons* ——

*The saying is sure and worthy of full acceptance. For to this end we
toil and struggle, because we have our hope set on the living God, who
is the savior of all people, especially of those who believe. These are
the things you must insist on and teach.*

−1 Timothy 4:9-11

*I lift up my eyes to the hills—from where will my help come?
My help comes from the Lord, who made heaven and earth.*

*He will not let your foot be moved; he who keeps you will not slumber.
He who keeps Israel will neither slumber nor sleep.*

*The Lord is your keeper; the Lord is your shade at your right hand.
The sun shall not strike you by day, nor the moon by night.*

*The Lord will keep you from all evil; he will keep your life.
The Lord will keep your going out and your coming in
from this time on forevermore.*

−Psalm 121

E ach semester, I begin teaching business ethics by holding up a large sheet of paper with a dark smudge on it. I ask the students, "What is this? What do you see?" Some say it's a bat. Other's say a bull's-eye that drips a little bit. Still others say a bird. Actually, it is a big sheet of white paper with a smudge on it. Most don't see the white paper. They focus on the aberration, the dark smudge, that which is contrary.

You and I live in a leaner time than we used to live in. I know that, and I know that all of you know that. Caution is urged at every turn. Life is unfair, and we may pay a heavy price for the greed and shortsightedness of people beyond our control.

The Scriptures tell us that when the prophet Jeremiah heard that the end of his world as he had known it was coming, the Babylonians were at the city gate, and the economy of his country was ruined. Yet he went and bought a piece of property in his hometown as a sign of his hope for the future.

It's an amazing conclusion to a poignant story. Jeremiah is in prison for speaking God's word, which irritated the King. There in prison, God warns him that his cousin, named Hanamel, is coming to sell Jeremiah a piece of the family's property. Now, Jeremiah's family had plotted to kill him, so it is doubtful that Hanamel has come to see Jeremiah out of the kindness of his heart. Hanamel wants to make some money off his cousin Jeremiah and flee. Jeremiah is totally aware of the bad days to come and knows the exile will be long and hard. Besides, he is in prison. Even if the land is useful, it is doubtful Jeremiah will ever get to see it and make use of it. So what does Jeremiah do? Listen to him as Scripture quotes him, *"And I bought the field at Anathoth from Hanamel my cousin, and weighed out the money to him, seventeen shekels of silver."* (32:9)

On the surface, this has got to be the worst real estate transaction recorded in the whole Bible. Hanamel, running away from that prison with the money in his hand, for selling the family farm in the face of the possession of the country by the Babylonian army, must have been the happiest real estate agent in history. He probably thought what P.T. Barnham expressed many centuries later, "There is a sucker born every minute."

Why does Jeremiah buy the field and preserve the documents? The answers are in his message: *"For thus says the Lord of hosts, the God of Israel—Houses and fields and vineyards shall again be bought on this land."* (32:15)

Jeremiah does not buy the land for its immediate value or for its investment potential. He buys it so his people will see his hope in God and his belief in a powerful and good God. He wants the people, not unlike my efforts with my students, to see that the long-term good is bigger than the stain of the present moment.

How can some people, like Jeremiah, bear up under the personal and social tragedies that take place in our world? How can people sing of God in the midst of natural disasters, a downturn in the economy, blatant human greed, and political incompetence that destroy their jobs and some of their aspirations? How can humans play symphonies of joy in the midst of tough and sometimes horrific situations? In 1992, the Associated Press circulated around the world a story headlined "The Cellist of Sarajevo." The tiny country of Bosnia was caught up in a civil war between the Bosnians and the Serbs. The beautiful capital city of Sarajevo, which had only eight years earlier been host of the Winter Olympic Games, was being relentlessly shelled by Serbian mortars, artillery guns, and airplanes. On May 27, a long line of people stood in front of a bakery at 4 p.m. A mortar shell made a direct hit on that line, instantly killing 22 of those people.

Across the street from the bakery, Vedron Smailovic witnessed the carnage from the window of his apartment. Vedron, a former cellist with the Sarajevo Symphony, resolved to do what he did best. When the debris and the bodies had been swept away, he put on his formal attire, a tuxedo with tails, picked up his cello, and walked out of his apartment. He placed a plastic chair by the huge crater the blast had created, and he played magnificent music for hours as bombs dropped on the city. For each of 22 days, one day for each victim, at precisely 4 p.m., he did the same thing. He played to the abandoned streets; he played to the burning buildings; he played to the terrified people who hid in their cellars as the bullets flew and the bombs burst.

There amid the rubble and the carnage of war, he made a courageous stand for human dignity, for compassion, and for peace. He pulled those around him upward and did not let the circumstances mute his hopes and the best that he knew how to do and to be.[8] Vedron Smailovic gave his people in Sarajevo an upward pull. He kept them familiar with the good; he kept them attuned to the authentic, the lasting promises of life so they would not be overwhelmed by the counterfeit things around them.

In 2009, a rare incident took place in aviation history. Charlotte, North Carolina Flight 1549 made a forced landing in the Hudson River in New York after losing power in both engines. All 155 people on board were rescued. Much of America watched the news about it, and many saw the flight crew parade across the field at the Super Bowl the same year.

The night after the incident happened, 20 members of the

National Transportation Safety Board's "Go Team" flew to New York. When the chairwoman of the group arrived, she was bombarded by questions from the press: "There are so many of you. And you got here so quickly. It's amazing. We have never seen so many of you investigating an incident. Are you trying to rule out a terrorist assault? Are you trying to get evidence of birds or multiple engine failure or fuel leaks?" The woman was silent. Finally, she held up her hands for them to be silent, and this is what she said: "You don't understand. We all raced here so quickly because this is the first chance we have ever had to study a situation where *everybody did it right*. That's what we are here to study. That's what will guide our training techniques for years to come. Everybody got it right in their response, and we need to study that more in depth than anything because you rarely get to study that."

She is correct—from the pilot to the crew to the passengers to the divers to the boat drivers to the emergency technicians to the ambulance drivers, everybody got it right; and instead of a perfect storm, there was a perfect peace.

Learning about life according to the scriptures seems to be a matter of focus, of looking up higher than your own self, of trying to get everything right in terms of attitude and perspective. Jesus once said, "If I be lifted up I will draw all people unto me." In like manner, the Psalmist declared, "I will lift up my eyes to the hills." Apparently, there is a law of the upward pull and the downward drift that operates in life.

I'm not a physicist or even a mathematician. But I do know this. You can take four apples and place one on each corner of a table. Tie a piece of string about three feet long to the stem of each apple. Gather the loose ends of the strings in your hand and raise your hand above the table until the strings become tight. As you tighten the strings by pulling upward, the apples will all come together. Essentially, says Scripture, when men and women pull upward, it's not just an individual phenomenon. All men and women are brought closer together in love and service when we lift up Christ,[9] when Christ lifts us up, and when we dream of a Kingdom where the lion and the lamb lie together, and every tear is wiped dry and every hurt is healed, not just in heaven but on earth.

How do we distinguish the fake, the false, and the counterfeit, from the real? We become so familiar with the authentic that we are never again fooled by the false. We practice the law of the upward pull. We look up. Our upward vision of God in Jesus Christ can become strength to our weary feet and a light on our meandering path.

There are also people in life whose hatred can drift us downward into their own cycle of vengeance. There are emotions of violence that can drift us downward into destroying our own family. There are seeds of ignorance and prejudice that can drift us downward into bigoted religious emotionalism. But there are also people in life who can pull us up through Jesus to God's perspective on our world. We can tap into sources of high emotions, worthy thoughts, and noble dreams that began before our birth and will outlive our own death.

We need some optimism in these days. We need it from our old folks, and we need it from our young folks. Not naiveté, not blind faith, but optimism. It really does not help our society to have inflammatory arguments about politics like we see on television.

If the only way we can transform ourselves is to destroy somebody else, that is not the birth of a new creation as sons and daughters of God.

How can people sing of God in the midst of natural disasters, a downturn in the economy, blatant human greed, and political incompetence that destroy their jobs and some of their aspirations? How can humans play symphonies of joy in the midst of tough and sometimes horrific situations? You start with yourself at any age. You become the person in your home, your office, your neighborhood, and your family who pulls everyone else up. It doesn't always have to be grandmother who pulls everyone up. You can help do some of the heavy lifting yourself.

One day, long after you are gone from this earth, you will want those who follow you in life to have a glimpse of how you got something right and pulled others up.

PART THREE

— The Sweet, Sweet Water Of Home —

A Place Where We
Are Known

—— *the lessons* ——

He entered the synagogue and for three months spoke out boldly, and argued persuasively about the kingdom of God. When some stubbornly refused to believe and spoke evil of the Way before the congregation, he left them, taking the disciples with him, and argued daily in the lecture hall of Tyrannus. This continued for two years, so that all the residents of Asia, both Jews and Greeks, heard the word of the Lord.

—Acts 19:8-10

"Do not let your hearts be troubled. Believe in God, believe also in me. In my father's house there are many dwelling places. If it were not so, would I have told you that I go to prepare a place for you? And if I go and prepare a place for you, I will come again and will take you to myself, so that where I am, there you may be also. And you know the way to the place where I am going." Thomas said to him, "Lord, we do not know where you are going. How can we know the way?"

—John 14:1-5

C hildhood is an exciting time. But, occasionally, it can have its boring moments. Some of those boring moments come when you are forced to do something that your parents enjoy doing but you do not.

My sister and I always dreaded "the Sunday afternoon drive." Our parents loved to herd both of us into the car with them for long, slow drives around the city looking at houses. They would sit in the front of the car, and my sister and I would be in the back seat. Oh, those were *long afternoons* for us children. Our parents never moved to another house. They just liked to look and dream. I have no idea if they felt frustrated or disappointed over where we lived. They never spoke much as we rode silently and slowly all around the areas in our city. "The Sunday afternoon ride to look at houses" was a staple of our existence, regardless of the dispositions of us children. It was also an exercise in social dreaming among the adults in our economic bracket.

Today, in our city, many adults my age love to spend their Sunday afternoons relaxing and reading and drinking coffee at Barnes and Noble. When my wife goes shopping, whether in High Point or another city, she likes to park me at a Barnes and Noble. It's like Barnes and Noble is my babysitter.

One Sunday, we were down in Durham, North Carolina, and I was dutifully ensconced in a comfortable chair in the Barnes and Noble at South Point Mall. I looked up and studied a young man who was intently reading and taking copious notes at a table next to me. He appeared to be in his late 20's. He was reading a book titled, "Fifty Fabulous Places To Raise Your Family." This guy was really into it. He was writing on legal pads that were spread out over the tabletop. He had listed the names of over 30 cities and had developed eight columns of information beside each city. After working for over an hour, he folded his research, put it in his briefcase, and left the store.

Is that how you find a good home? Is that also how one finds a good college to attend? Is it the city? Is it the quality of the people who live near you there? Is it the quality of the housing you live in? Can you discover it from reading a book of statistics or getting on the internet and looking at university homepages? I have often wondered if that young man and his wife found a fabulous place to raise their family. Or *were they disappointed?*

Jesus, according to John, mentions the image of a house being prepared for his followers in the place where God dwells. Jesus uses the image of being in God's house with many dwelling places to explain how we reside in the eternal presence of God. The apostle Paul, too, states that joining with Jesus in the presence of God means entering the *house* that God has provided in heaven for eternity. Now, for most people, believing in God is complicated enough. Why do Jesus and Paul complicate things further with the *house* image?

Jesus, in His earthly existence, didn't seem to think much of houses. The homes of people, as well as houses of worship, held little appeal for Him. He was born in a manger. He said that the son of man is homeless and has no place to lay his head. On another occasion, when he and his disciples entered the city, the disciples were impressed by the size of the temple. But Jesus was unimpressed with the huge building. He told them that the stone the builders rejected was the cornerstone of God's house.

Paul also was unimpressed with houses. He was a tent maker, and the early church met everywhere. We read in Acts 19 that Paul used the lecture hall of Tyrannus in Ephesus for two years as his church there. The New Revised Standard Version of the Bible contains a footnote that records that Paul occupied the lecture hall from eleven in the morning until four in the afternoon. Paul used as his church a gymnasium, a public building, erected in the name of a Roman man named Tyrannus who probably gave the city government lots of money to put his name on it. Houses and where the church met were just not that important to Paul and the early Christians. Certainly, a lecture hall was not a place conducive for worship and starting a church.[1] Apparently, any building would do.

Why then do Jesus and Paul give us the image of a house as our eternal home? The meaning of living now and forever in the house of God is a special thing for you and me, especially in times when we remember deceased friends and family members. We often need to hold to the belief that God not only created us, but that same God lays for us the foundations of an eternal home.

To understand the difference between the Christian God and the gods of ancient Rome and Greece, we need to understand the difference between a house and a temple. Greek temples were designed as houses for the god or goddess to whom they were dedicated. No humans went inside the temple. That was where the gods lived. The worshippers stood outside the buildings and at best got to walk around in a central room. Temples were for gods, and humans stood outside and made their appeals for favors from there on the porch. There was no sense of any special relationship between those gods and humanity.

For Christians, a church is a place of fellowship between God and humanity. God has become one with us through Jesus, and God not only knows our name, but builds us a house to live in and to meet God in. In a world that viewed a religious house as a place where humans stood on the porch and begged for favors, the Christians depicted God as laying out the floorplans and elevations for each of us to live in a house constructed for us by God who also lives there with us. The residents of God's houses are people, and Paul and Jesus insist upon the point. Resurrection is going from an earthly tent to a divine mansion.[2]

A key to understanding John 14 is to believe that our God is a personal God. To encounter Jesus is to encounter God. The whole message of the gospel of John is the assertion that God knows our name and prepares a personal place for each of us to live eternally with God. John quotes Jesus as saying, *"I am the good shepherd; I know my own sheep and they know me . . ."* (10:14). In a world of much loneliness and despair, that is a profound message. God loves each of us as if there were only one of us to love. We are all a valued part of the heavenly kingdom.

Oscar Hammerstein said, "A bell's not a bell till you ring it, and a song's not a song until you sing it." A faith in God is not a faith in God until you share it. There is not a single book in the Bible that was written to an individual. Every book in the Bible was written to a group. Religion itself is a set of beliefs and practices that help a group of people face its ultimate problems of life and death. Something positive happens when we talk to one another face-to-face and share our faith. Even in our world of e-mails, teleconferencing, DVDs, and text messaging, when human beings personally deliver to us words of faith and hope through their voices, their faces, their eyes, their gestures, and their touches, something special happens.

Jesus' words make their way gently to us across the chasms of recorded time: "Come to me all of you who are heavy laden and I will give you rest . . . Do not let your hearts be troubled . . . In my father's house are many dwelling places . . . I go to prepare a place for you." Obviously, our God knows who we are and where we belong.

Being the Dean of the Chapel at High Point University, I have been involved in offering worship services for parents and alumni on a number of family weekends. At the beginning of the year, I jokingly tell the new students, "Don't worry, if your parents come back for family weekend, I will pretend I know you very well."

The real essence of Jesus' message is the assertion that when it comes to knowing God and God knowing us, God does not have to pretend. We can rest easy. Our God knows who we are. That knowledge should empower us to reach out to others in assurance and hope, and remember to stay close to the source of our redemption.

Staying Close to the Source

—— *the lessons* ——

"I know your works; you are neither cold nor hot. I wish that you were either cold or hot. So, because you are luke warm, and neither cold nor hot, I am about to spit you out of my mouth. For you say, 'I am rich, I have prospered, and I need nothing.' You do not realize that you are wretched, pitiable, poor, blind, and naked. Therefore I counsel you to buy from me gold refined by fire so that you may be rich; and white robes to clothe you and to keep the shame of your nakedness from being seen; and salve to anoint your eyes so that you may see. I reprove and discipline those whom I love. Be earnest, therefore, and repent. Listen! I am standing at the door, knocking; if you hear my voice and open the door, I will come in to you and eat with you, and you with me."

–Revelation 3:15-20

One of the two who heard John speak and followed him was Andrew, Simon Peter's brother. He first found his brother Simon and said to him, "We have found the Messiah" (which is translated Anointed). He brought Simon to Jesus, who looked at him and said, "You are Simon son of John. You are to be called Cephas" (which is translated Peter).

The next day Jesus decided to go to Galilee. He found Philip and said to him, "Follow me." Now Philip was from Bethsaida, the city of Andrew and Peter.

–John 1:40-44

One of Hollywood's finest movie producers, A.C. Lyles, was a very close friend to former President Ronald Reagan. He regularly attended White House meetings with President Reagan and his staff, and he also functioned as a Hollywood liaison, getting celebrities to entertain at the White House and other presidential functions. He tells a story about an event in the White House that you'll never read about in the newspaper.[3]

A.C. was having a friendly conversation in the Oval Office with President Reagan during the waning days of his last term in office. He noticed that the President kept working on something. Finally, he asked him what he was doing. The President told him he was filling out the paperwork so he could obtain a California driver's license when he returned home from being President.

A.C. couldn't believe what he was seeing. "You haven't driven a car in years, and when you get home the Secret Service will still be driving you everywhere you go. Why do you think you'll need a driver's license?" President Reagan looked up at his friend A.C. and said, "Well, I thought I might need it for identification." Can you imagine someone so prominent being afraid of being unrecognized among strangers?

A church should be a place where we feel recognized in one another's presence because of our common identity as children of God. All the people with whom we worship are not just strangers who happened to find themselves in the same place.

Some years ago, a professor from Boston College and I led a group of 35 people on a study tour of Greece. Most of the people were from High Point, North Carolina, and Boston, Massachusetts. We flew to Athens, and after three days there, a huge Mercedes bus pulled up to our hotel to take us on an arduous seven day bus ride. We went first to Corinth, where teenagers were selling shirts with the Apostle Paul's picture on them. We looked at the sites where Paul had been in prison. We held a service in the synagogue ruins where he had preached. We rode in the bus, and we walked around many cities. It was hot, dreadfully hot, even for Greece.

Tourists were everywhere, snapping pictures and traipsing over the ancient ruins. Twenty or more tour buses would be parked in a line everywhere we stopped. We found ourselves in the same places with thousands of tourists. Religious books and trinkets, holy rocks and video and audio tapes, t-shirts and even bottles of holy water were for sale at every turn.

Finally, on day six, we were all riding the bus from the Peloponnesian area in Southwest Greece up to cross the isthmus by ferry and go to Olympia to see the stadium where the first Olympics were held. As we were driving alongside the ocean, we were just one more tour bus in a long line of other buses going toward the ferry. A lady from High Point came up to the front and spoke to me and the bus driver.

"Does every tour bus stop at the same places?" she inquired.

"Oh, yes," said the Greek driver. "Everyone wants to see Athens, all the places where Paul preached about Jesus, and also where the Olympic Games were held, at Olympia and Delphi."

"Well, I'm tired of seeing all this history," she stated. "I'm tired of being shoved around by all these strangers. I've learned a great deal," she conceded, "but I don't need to see any more ruins and buy any more trinkets. We can't even agree on a place to eat half the time. Isn't there somewhere we can go and just rest?"

The driver stopped the bus. He looked at her and said, "Well, we can make a right turn here and go to my hometown of Patras. We are proud of it. No tourists go there. It is about a few kilometers off the tour route. We think it is a great place because it is the place where Andrew was crucified by the Romans. He is the one who brought his brother, Peter, to meet Jesus. His church is still there."

Quickly, the lady collected five dollars from each of us, gave it to the driver, and said, "Hang a right."

As you might know, Andrew was crucified on an X-shaped cross. When we approached the city, we were amazed to see that virtually every store we passed had an X-shaped cross in its window. As we turned a corner past the hustle and bustle of the noonday crowd, there was this huge church of St. Andrew with its golden dome, right in the middle of the work-a-day world. It was immaculate. The white walls were luminous, and the stained glass windows were beautiful as the sun shone through them. The floor was so clean you could eat off it. The round chandelier that hung down from the golden dome illuminated a huge floor to ceiling mural behind the altar. The mural depicted Andrew introducing his brother Peter to Jesus.

To the right of the altar was a circular room completely lit with candles. People were sitting in chairs around a silver container on a table and lighting the candles around it. Behind the container was a metallic frame in the shape of an X cross. It was full of candles. After meditating for a moment, people would get up and light one of the candles on that cross and leave. Our group sat in silence, in complete awe for many minutes among the Greek people, listening to their prayers in a language we did not recognize. Yet we understood their depth and spirit. A Greek widow, dressed in black, which signified that she had lost a husband in World War II, smiled a rather toothless smile at me.

"American?" she asked.

I nodded.

"Me speak a little English," she said.

Then she leaned over and whispered, "Andrew was a good man."

One by one, we passengers from the tour bus lit a candle and filed out. No one said anything for quite a while. It had been such a spiritual and meaningful experience.

We stopped and ate lunch in the city, feeling not like tourists, but like family as we conversed with the natives in broken English and gestured toward the church rising off in the distance. It was what we had in common, a faith that transcended our lifestyles, our intellects, and our differences. In fact, we well-fed and comparatively wealthy Americans felt poor in comparison to what those peasants had in the realm of their spirits.

There were no t-shirts for sale; no postcards; no religious books. Not a soul in our group had dared even take a picture. No one needed to take a picture—we had been to the source of our faith. Today, over 25 years later, when I encounter people who were on that three week tour of Greece, they point to the experience at the Church of St. Andrew as their most meaningful remembrance of the entire trip. As we drove away that day from Patras, I had asked the bus driver, "Why do you reason that the tourist buses don't come here?"

"It's not commercialized," he stated. "Tourists mainly want to buy souvenirs and books for themselves and have pictures taken so their friends will be impressed. *Many would feel uncomfortable in the presence of the real thing.* But I knew you people would not."

He reminded us of the necessity of staying close to the source of many of our blessings and our common humanity as we intellectually broaden our horizons, expand our families, and enrich our personal lives.

One of the clearest spiritual illusions used by the early Christians was the church at Laodicea. Quite frankly, the situation at Laodicea strongly resembled many a modern American scene. Laodicea was one of the wealthiest cities in the world. A famous medical center was located there that had gained quite a reputation for its scientific research. The scientists in Laodicea had produced eye salve and ear ointments that were world famous. The people who lived and studied there were under the illusion that material wealth equaled spiritual health. All the scientific, educational, and political facilities were up to date and first class! And the religious life in Laodicea was so tolerant that it was meaningless. Those who believed in emperor worship and pagan mystery religions meshed with Jews and Christians in a common philosophy of money making.

The Laodiceans were proud of their accomplishments, took delight in their intellectual prowess, and looked forward to lives of greater financial promise than those who did not reside in Laodecia. They had safety, science, wealth, and freedom. But that was it.

The Scripture from Revelation hits the situation head on: The Laodiceans thought they were smarter than they really were, wealthier than they really were, and healthier than they really were. Their science, their wealth, their health, and their intelligence were not put in a proper perspective. Their souls were lost. They had become lukewarm.

About six miles from Laodicea was the city of Hierapolis. This city had hot springs that were great for healing bodies. The hot water flowed to Laodicea and came down a waterfall over a cliff just across from the city. By the time the water reached Laodicea, it was lukewarm and would gag anyone who tried to drink it.

The Scripture is referring to water that has traveled so far from its source that it is no longer being used for its original purpose, healing baths. Lukewarm doesn't mean a lack of activity. It means getting so far away from the *source* of your wealth, from the *source* of your health, from the *source* of our intelligence, that we forget the original healing potential of our life.

When Jesus gave us the great purpose of life as "to love God with all your body, mind, and soul and to love your neighbor as yourself," his meaning was quite clear.

Our wealth should make us charitable. Our science should be used to benefit, not destroy, humankind. Our accomplishments should make us humble. And our knowledge should take us by the hand and keep us comfortable in the presence of the real thing, the one who created us.

With its steeple pointed upward, a church reminds us that the *source* of all beauty, the *source* of all wealth, the *source* of all intelligence, and the *source* of all life is the creator God, whose presence and love were made known to us through Jesus the Christ.

Remembering Whose We Are

— *the lesson* —

No, in all these things we are more than conquerors through him who loved us. For I am convinced that neither death, nor life, nor angels, nor rulers, nor things present, nor things to come, nor powers, nor height, nor depth, nor anything else in all creation, will be able to separate us from the love of God in Christ Jesus our Lord.

–Romans 8:37-39

E very Fourth of July, we Americans rightly celebrate the *power* of our forebears in this land to achieve under God the formation of a nation and to win their freedom from being ruled by the British. We certainly, as Christians, believe that God gives power to God's special and needy people. From age to age, the perspective is the same: God is powerful, and we need to ask God to give us some power, as well.

The nation Israel, at one point, viewed God as a deity who would take all God could stomach of human nature, let Israel's enemies push her almost to the brink and then knock everything off the wall and start over. At other times, God would take a lot of irritation from Israel herself. Then God would use another nation to knock Israel off the wall so she could learn a lesson.

One of the critical issues in the ministry of Jesus Christ was the issue of power. Jesus contended that most of us do not understand the way God uses power. Jesus was afraid that we humans would forget or fail to grasp the nature of the God who really owns us. We often ask, "Why does this powerful God allow so much evil in the world? Why doesn't this God do things differently? While all those Jews and Christians were praying, why didn't God strike down Hitler much sooner? Why didn't God take out Osama bin

Laden before September 11, 2001?"

I would have if I had been God. But Jesus Christ maintained that "God is love." God bears our grief and carries our sorrows: not just at Calvary but all the time. That is certainly a sobering thought. It means that God's power is directed toward a purpose: the whole world coming to understand that love is greater than force. As such, if love is God's goal, God cannot rush to God's end by using any possible means.

Well, then, what power comes to me as a human being when I pray to God? What does prayer do for me? What power can I claim? Certainly, one positive aspect of prayer is that prayer puts us in touch with an identity that began before our birth and continues after our death. Prayer helps us remember to whom we belong. And this is especially important for us who live in the United States. We are expected, because of our heritage, to have higher values than the rest of the world. To whom much power is given, much responsibility is expected. The world expects us to act Christian, and that is often quite a burden.

It is amazing how human beings can lose their identity. To forget who you are is called *amnesia*. I'll never forget the time in college that one of my teammates on the Furman University football team forgot who he was. He was the biggest athlete recruited in my class at Furman University, and he played tackle on the offensive line. Since our colors were purple and white, we had purple helmets with a big white stripe down them. That is, everybody but him. His head was so big that he could not wear one of our helmets. The Riddell Helmet Company had to make one especially for him, and it was a white helmet. He looked funny out there in his white helmet while all the others were purple.

One day, he did not come to class. Then a week passed with no one seeing him. Nothing in his room was out of order. His bed was made and his clothes were all there, even his wallet. He had just disappeared. Police throughout the South searched for him.

His picture was on the news on television every night. Three weeks later, the Atlanta police found him walking around the streets of downtown Atlanta. He didn't know who he was. He had amnesia. Nobody knew how he got there or where he stayed or how he had eaten. They took him back to South Carolina and reintroduced him to his family. They said, "Meet your Momma and your Daddy. This is where you came from." He shrugged his shoulders and replied, "I don't know those people."

Fortunately, after a year, his memory gradually returned. He remembered who he was and came back to finish college. He didn't forget who he was anymore, and he eventually graduated.

It must be a horrible thing to forget who you are. Fred Craddock believes that we humans have a residue of our memory of the Garden of Eden. We have a faint reminiscence of closeness to God. We are all born, created, with this faint memory in our minds. In essence, prayer gives us the power to tie ourselves to an identity that precedes our birth and extends beyond our death. We are enrolled in a story that is greater than our personal story. The roots of who we are lie with the ancient Jews. From them came Jesus the Christ. If we do not absorb all that into our awareness, our identity is not complete, and we are left orphaned in the 21st century.

It is amazing how quickly we human beings can forget that we are children of God and should live by love instead of force. I've forgotten those points at times in my life and had to be reintroduced to my Christian heritage. It happens all the time. We get orphaned without any memory of our heritage. There have been some horrible cases of amnesia in our own history.

Perhaps one of the worst cases occurred before we even became a nation. Consider the bloodiest war ever fought on American soil. It is known as King Phillip's War. In 1621, the Pilgrims were greeted by an Indian leader named Massasoit. Without Massasoit's help, the Pilgrims would never have survived that first year. In like manner, Massasoit realized from the start that his own fortunes and future were linked to those of the foreigners in his land. The Indians and the English lived together for 55 years. It wasn't easy. It was 55 years of compromise and struggle. Often, there were harrowing give and takes from both sides. As long as both sides remembered that they needed each other, there was peace. The next generation forgot their heritage.

Philip was the son of Massasoit. In 1675, Philip went to war.[4] The fragile bonds that had held the strangers together for decades had been irreparably broken. The lives of the Native and English people had been so intertwined that many faced a dilemma. Some Indians supported Philip; others joined the colonial forces; still others tried to stay out of it altogether. King Philip's war only lasted 14 months, but it was bloody. The entire region became a killing ground. One-third of the more than 100 towns in New England were burned and abandoned. Ten percent of the 70,000 people in New England lost their lives in the 14 months of the war. In terms of percentage of population killed, King Philip's War was more than twice as bloody as the American Civil War and more than seven times as lethal as the American Revolution. And that doesn't count the number of Indians who ended the war as slaves. Since the fighting caught everyone by surprise, what happened?

When violence and fear grip a society, there is an urge to demonize the enemy. The English and Indians began to view their former neighbors as evil and subhuman. Amazingly, in this deadliest war in American history, heroes existed on both sides who remembered a different past. Some English believed the Indians were not inherently evil, and there were some Indians who believed the same about the English. These were the people who finally brought the war to an end.

It was their descendants who helped pave the way for the creation of higher values, and a thirst for freedom and unity among the colonies 100 years later that produced this grand old flag that stood and still stands for a higher way of life. Those descendants lived together, fought together, and some died together to win freedom. You can judge a country by how well she remembers her past and passes along to others the lessons she has learned. America has learned, hopefully, how to shine as a beacon of higher values.

You can tell the values of a country by how many people are trying to get into it and how many people are trying to leave it. There are not many trying to leave our country, and there never will be as long as we remember whose we are.

One of my dearest friends is a man named Charles E. Merrill, Jr. His father founded Merrill-Lynch. Charles is 93 years old, as I share this with readers, and is still living on Beacon Hill in Boston. I called Wednesday to make sure he is still alive. We used to take long walks once a month around Boston and talk. Charles never entered the brokerage business because he chose to spend his entire career giving the company's money away. So they let his brother run the business and let Charles give away most of what it earned. On one of our walks, I said to Charles, "So many people in this country have benefited from your trust. Why did you become such a giver?" He told me a war story of his own.

He said he was in the Army in the infantry and was over in Belgium. His outfit was engaged in ferocious fighting with the Germans. Charles got lost from his outfit and was slowly moving along in an open area in hilly terrain, holding his gun down by his side. As he started up a hill, a German panzer tank rolled up and over the hill and stopped in front of him. It scared him so much he dropped his rifle. He froze. The turret swung the cannon around straight at him. A cover opened on the side, and a German soldier popped up behind a machine gun, which he cocked and pointed straight at Charles' head. Immediately, the top hatch of the panzer popped open, as well. The tank commander yelled down to the gunner who looked back up at him. The commander stood there for a moment, surveyed the situation, and in Charles' words, "It was like he remembered who he was." He shook his finger at his subordinate, like a displeased elementary school teacher at a child, and motioned ahead. Then both of them slammed the covers down. The tank backed up about ten feet and turned right and then left and went completely around Charles and kept going.

Ah, I thought, foxhole religion—Charles got so scared he made a promise to God to give all his money away for letting him live. But that wasn't the case. When Charles returned to the States after the war, he realized that his father had left him a weapon more powerful to help or harm people than a Panzer tank—a lot of money. He told me that he loved this great country, America, that gave so many people weapons for healing and assisting others. He was determined to be responsible with his weapons and remember who he was, just as that enemy tank commander had done. He, like the German before him, realized that he was born into a situation he could not control. All he could do was be responsible with those things he could control. The American flag helps us remember the high standard of living that we have and those who have fought and continue to fight for us to have it. We should thank God for those people every day. The *Christian* flag helps us remember whose we are and how we should use that high standard of living.

The disciples went to Jesus one day and asked, "Teach us to pray. It seems to give you a power we don't have." It was one of the few things they ever asked of Jesus. And Jesus told them how to do it. You just say—give us, forgive us, and deliver us. Give us our daily bread. The daily bread of America is freedom, peace, and love toward all; forgive us as we forgive others—our nation has been a forgiving nation and still needs to be; we rebuild the countries we fight against; and there are some deeds for which we need to be forgiven; deliver us from evil. There are some things that are beyond our individual and even national abilities to deal with—diseases, enemies, horrible genocides and starvations—that we just have to pray to God for deliverance from. But Paul is right in the use of his paired opposites:

> neither death, nor life
> nor angels, nor powers
> nor things present, nor things to come
> neither powers from on high, nor powers from below
> nor height, nor depth
> nor any other creature—shall ever be able to separate us from the love of God.

A Tale Of Two Parties

— *t h e   l e s s o n s* —

*Six days before the Passover Jesus came to Bethany, the home of
Lazarus, whom he had raised from the dead. There they gave a dinner
for him. Martha served, and Lazarus was one of those at the table with
him. Mary took a pound of costly perfume made of pure nard, anointed
Jesus' feet, and wiped them with her hair. The house was filled with the
fragrance of the perfume. But Judas Iscariot, one of his disciples (the one
who was about to betray him), said, "Why was this perfume not sold for
three hundred denarii and the money given to the poor?" (He said this
not because he cared about the poor, but because he was a thief; he kept
the common purse and used to steal what was put into it.) Jesus said,
"Leave her alone. She bought it so that she might keep it for the day
of my burial."*

–John 12:1-7

*A dispute also arose among them as to which one of them was to
be regarded as the greatest. But he said to them, "The king of the
Gentiles lord it over them; and those in authority over them are called
benefactors. But not so with you; rather the greatest among you must
become like the youngest, and the leader like the one who serves. For
who is greater, the one who is at the table or the one who serves? Is it
not the one at the table? But I am among you as one who serves."*

–Luke 22:24-27

Most people, me included, love a good party. As Dean of the Chapel at High Point University, my preaching audience is composed almost entirely of college students, and they really love to party. College students are detached from their parents and tossed headlong into a nightly environment peopled almost exclusively by persons their own age. Their parents worry about this. When high school seniors tour any college campus, their parents have a question deep inside them that frequently shivers its way to your ears when they get ready to depart after a campus visit. The question isn't about the curriculum or the class sizes or the composition of the student body. Sometimes, the question is an afterthought, and other times it is a direct, frontal attack: "Uh, is this a *party* school?"

Most of the time, the college tour guide will begin a verbal tap dance. "What, our school? Noooo way. Well-planned Student Life activities fill the calendar. Outstanding cultural events abound. Our library stays open 24 hours. The campus is wireless so students can continue to work away on their subjects even after they leave the library. Your student will be too busy to party." Most parents don't buy that for a moment. They know their children better than that.

You and I live in an age of speed and rapid communication. Forget the telephone, e-mail, and federal express. There is
no more rapid fire transmission of information than the word
that gets around town among high school students when someone's parents are going to be out of town for the weekend. Forget
the new math. I still can't explain how 74 teenagers could, on a
Saturday night, sneak into our family hot tub, which was designed
to hold eight people, or how over 300 young people could cram
into a small vacant lot at midnight. At Easter time, many churches
focus on Jesus' last seven words from the cross. Many a parent's
plaintive scream has been these last seven words: "We only left
town for one night!"

Jesus of Nazareth apparently loved parties, too. He performed
his first miracle at a wedding reception in Cana. He was accused by
his enemies of being a glutton and a drinker because he socialized
with many different types of people. He spoke of the Kingdom of
God as a banquet hall and of God as one who would kill a fatted
calf and throw a big party when prodigal sinners came to their
senses and returned home.

Scripture records that there were actually two last supper gath-
erings in Jesus' final week on this earth. One was his last supper
with his friends that the writers of the gospels of John, Matthew
and Mark said took place in Bethany.[5] The other was his last supper
with his disciples, his professional colleagues, in Jerusalem. A final
party with friends is much different from a final party with your
co-workers. The former is a real joy. The latter can be a real chore,
both for you and the guests.

When Diane and I moved back South in 1982 from Massachusetts, two last-week going away parties were held for us, one with
friends and the other with colleagues. One of my dearest friends
is a man named Peter Gomes. Many people know him by his best-
selling work, *The Good Book*. It is an insightful analysis of the Bible.
But to a few of us, he is known as the giver of great parties. His

magnificent home, Sparks House, sits right in the middle of the Harvard University campus. It is decorated with antiques and has been featured in *Better Homes and Gardens* magazine. My last month on the job at Harvard, Peter said to me, "Harold, I want to give you and Diane a party. Invite 20 friends from the University. We'll have it at my house. You tell me what you'd like to have to eat and drink, and we'll have a splendid evening." Indeed, it was quite a party. It began early in the evening and concluded well into the next day. The laughter and stories flew wildly throughout the evening. People freely talked about their colleagues and certain university experiences in ways that could never be repeated.

The next week, the official university good-bye party was held in the Dean's residence in the shape of a faculty-spouse formal dinner. Little speeches were given. The institution put its best foot forward. It was awkward and uncomfortable for me. I felt that half the people there couldn't wait to get me out the door so they could recommend one of their friends for my old job. The other half were probably jealous that they weren't leaving with me.

Last suppers with friends are radically different from last suppers with professional associates. We should not overlook the decision of three of the gospel writers to include *both* suppers held for Jesus. Apparently, there is as much about the Kingdom of God in the party for Jesus in Bethany as there is in the supper for Jesus in Jerusalem. The party in Bethany was held in the house of Mary and Martha. Their home was Jesus' favorite place to spend the night. His friends held an appreciation dinner for Jesus six days before the Passover, the day of the "official" religious dinner.

Mary and Martha were always making a fuss over Jesus. My guess is that at some point, the sisters had asked Jesus how they could ever repay him for what he had done for their brother, Lazarus. Jesus might have said, "What about one of those wonderful dinners you girls are famous for giving?"

"No problem." The party was on. Lazarus himself came to the

supper and was right there at the table with Jesus. Even Mary let down her hair. As Jesus was reclining at the table, she knelt and poured a pound of perfume on his bare feet. Then she did what no respectable woman in that day would ever do in public. She let down her hair and wiped Jesus' feet with it. Jesus' supper with his friends evoked an impulsive, emotional reaction from Mary. The perfume was worth an average year's salary to a common worker living in Palestine in those days. Imagine someone today taking a bottle of perfume that cost $31,900 and pouring it over the bare feet of a friend at a going-away party.

But remember, this is a last supper among *friends*. It was quite different from the last supper with the disciples, where a fight almost broke out over who was going to be favored in the kingdom of God. So different was this party that even the Gospels reshaped the party to make it fit their purpose.

Both parties are necessary. Both have grace in them, and both parties point toward the Kingdom of God. We are well aware that the last supper Jesus held with his disciples created words of instruction for the church. That kind of professional and institutional grace is important. The party in Jerusalem was done for the sake of the church, the institution. It's important for public institutions to remember the Christ and formally proclaim His death and resurrection. Institutions preserve and protect. The church's observance of the Lord's Supper in Jerusalem helps us do that. But what about the Lord's other last supper? What does the one in Bethany have to say to us?

I believe that supper is the one we also need to focus on. It speaks of the personal grace of God that is given to people who interact with one another and form a community of friends. Friends create community when they enjoy one another across their differences. Friends get lavish with their assets on one another. Friends can, figuratively speaking, raise one another from the dead in ways that institutions cannot. In fact, Mary, Martha, and Lazarus were not in attendance at the Last Supper in Jerusalem.

This, too, is an important message. Our world is headed away from friendships that span communities. We are moving into special interest groups. Special interest groups do not create community. Special interest groups emphasize our differences.

Mark Trotter[6] has traced what has happened in our society through the architecture of the private home. Before and through the mid-1940, homes in America were built with huge front porches. It was expected that people would sit on those porches and have a conversation with the community as its people walked by.

After World War II, the suburbs were the dominant places to live. In the suburbs, the family was moved from the front porch to the patio in the backyard. The community was scaled down to one's family and invited guests in a private location.

Later, as television became common, the family moved inside to the family room. The TV tray became a symbol for meals. The family sat around the television, shutting the rest of the world out.

Now, we have the final innovations, the computer and the cell phone. The computer is a solitary experience. Studies have shown that computers increase isolation. One sits at a screen and talks to people who possess similar interests across the world. A local community is not needed. In fact, we may even do most of our shopping and chatting over the Internet. One day, I fear, a party will simply be providing a room where people can go stand by themselves in nooks and corners and watch their iPhones and Blackberries and text message the same few people they have been messaging since high school.

Turning strangers into neighbors and neighbors into friends seems to be a pretty consistent theme in Jesus' life. To sit close in our seating arrangements and to be greeted by name with a hug is to feel close and joyous. We perhaps need the institutionalization, and denominationally focused machinations, of the larger churches to which we belong, to keep the gospel of Jesus Christ alive in these days of public relations campaigns. But we need places of closeness as well.

Figuratively speaking, we need more than Jerusalem. Jesus speaks to us in other ways. We also need Bethany, a place where strangers become friends and the trappings of the mighty give way to the joys of the simple. We need the enactment of an old proverb:

Better is a dinner of vegetables where love is

Than a fatted ox and hatred with it. (Proverbs 15:17)

Occasionally, we need to drink the sweet, sweet, water of home.

The Sweet, Sweet Water
Of Home

— *the lessons* —

David said longingly, "O that someone would give me water to drink from the well of Bethlehem that is by the gate!" Then the three warriors broke through the camp of the Philistines, drew water from the well of Bethlehem that was by the gate, and brought it to David. But he would not drink of it; he poured it out to the Lord, for he said, "The Lord forbid that I should do this. Can I drink the blood of the men who went at the risk of their lives?" Therefore he would not drink it.

—2 Samuel 23:15-17

A Samaritan woman came to draw water, and Jesus said to her, "Give me a drink." (His disciples had gone to the city to buy food.)

The woman said to him, "Sir, you have no bucket, and the well is deep. Where do you get that living water? Are you greater than our ancestor Jacob, who gave us the well, and with his sons and his flocks drank from it?" Jesus said to her, "Everyone who drinks of this water will be thirsty again, but those who drink of the water that I will give them will never be thirsty. The water that I will give will become in them a spring of water gushing up to eternal life." The woman said to him, "Sir, give me this water, so that I may never be thirsty or have to keep coming here to draw water."

—John 4:7-9, 11-15

One brisk day in February, I journeyed to Williamsburg, Virginia, to visit an old friend. Dave was the retired Chaplain of the Atlantic Fleet. Like most career military families, Dave and his wife had moved around a bit, from the United States to Asia and the Middle East, and many points in between. When they retired, they tried living in several cities near the Atlantic Ocean. Nowhere felt like home. Finally, they moved into a neat little home in Williamsburg.

They had just moved in when I visited them. Though slowed by age, they moved around with beaming faces. After lunch, we sat in their den talking about old times. I asked them, "How do you like it here?" His wife beamed and said, "This is the best water that we have ever had." Dave echoed her, "It sure is. The water here tastes so good!" I was puzzled. They had only moved three miles from their last residence and were on the same city water system.

On the drive back to High Point, I reflected on their words. "This is the best water we have ever had." At a deeper level, I think they were saying they were at peace and that they recognized the place they were living as their final home on this earth, which it turned out to be. They had finally found the sweet, sweet water of home.

My mother-in-law, in the last few years of her life, did not really know *where* she was living. She resided in an Alzheimer's Unit in Arbor Acres in Winston-Salem, North Carolina. When she was still able to talk and someone would mention her childhood hometown, Aiken, South Carolina, she would smile and say, "They have good water there."

Water is an important symbol of home because water is so vital to our survival. We were all conceived in water and nurtured by water. The book of Genesis depicts water as the substance of creation. The Spirit of God hovers over the waters of chaos and brings forth all life out of the water. And it is through the immersed or sprinkled water of baptism that we are established as Christians, loved and chosen by God.

One of the great stories in the Bible is the very last story told about King David before his death. David is now an old man. His life has gone downhill after bringing his nation the only real golden age it had ever known. He is one who had conspired to steal another man's wife. He lives with the sadness of having had a son plot against him.

Now, near the end of his days, the former great man is hiding in a cave not far from Bethlehem. He is at the edge of defeat, and his life has not turned out the way he had wanted it to turn out.

From his cave, David and his few remaining followers can look out and see Bethlehem, David's hometown, which is held by the Philistines. As old David eats the rancid military rations and drinks the stale, warm, flat, water from a goat-skin, he begins to reminisce about his childhood. As he remembers and drifts backward through the shadows of his childhood, he sees the fields where he played as a little boy; he remembers the village walls where he used to race with his friends; he particularly remembers the well by the gate where he drew the wonderful water of Bethlehem. But now, the town is in the hands of strangers; and he is old, and he is sick, and he is tired! He yearns for just a taste of Bethlehem's water. He utters, "*Oh, that someone would get me a drink of water from the well near the gate of Bethlehem, my hometown."*

Listening to David lament are three brave men who will do anything for the man they love. At the risk of their own lives, they slip through the Philistine lines and draw a jug of water from Bethlehem's well. With great pleasure, they give the old, dying king what he dreams of—the cold, clear water of his childhood. David is overwhelmed. But he realizes the cost is too much—three young people risking their lives because of his homesickness for the past. He will not use their bravery just to quench his own thirst. He takes the jug and pours the water on the ground.

Billionaire Warren Buffet acknowledges that money and power can give a person undue advantage over employees, partners, and others.[7] Buffet is fond of telling a story about the time his family had a dog on the roof, and his son called to the dog. The dog jumped and suffered a broken leg but lived. Out of that awful experience, Buffet learned not to take advantage of people who, like the dog, love you so much they will harm themselves to please you. Like old king David, he vowed never to put people into those situations.

I believe that at many points in life, all of us can identify with the danger of feeling thirsty and nostalgic outside the walls of our childhood. We may even long to walk through the buildings and schools and even the churches and secret places where we lived in our own little world as a child. But we see those places occupied by strangers. Sometimes our nostalgia for those old, simple times can drag those closest to us through a lot of danger to their own well-being as they try to satisfy us. Parents sometimes try to relive their childhood through the lives of their children, putting those children in danger of never finding their own destiny. Grandparents can do the same thing to their grandchildren. I hope I can avoid being like David and not let my nostalgia for old places and simple times become a savage beast to my children and my grandchildren who love me.

For instruction in living, I often read the story of Jesus and the lonely woman he met at a well one day. She was a Samaritan, and she had come to the well to draw water. It was potentially a danger-ous scene. Jesus was a Jew, and Jews were to have no dealings with Samaritans. It was a conversation that should never have happened at all. Men did not speak to women in public in that society. And Jews did not speak to Samaritans, period. The history of Jews and Samaritans was like that of many Jews and Muslims in Israel and Palestine. They hated each other religiously.

And this woman was a stereotype, a caricature of the enemy. She was immoral. She had had five husbands and was, at the time, living with someone to whom she was not married. In Jewish eyes, that made her chronically immoral.

The worst possible thing happened. *Jesus asked her for a drink of water.* In the Jewish culture, courtship rituals were carried out at wells. They were called "well betrothals." If a Jewish man spoke to a woman in public and asked that woman for a drink at a well and she gave it to him, they next had to go to her father, and the man had to ask for her hand in marriage. The woman was shocked. "How is it that you, a Jew, ask a drink of me, a woman of Samaria?"

This scene is, perhaps, the most revolutionary scene in the Bible. No one can miss the point. Jesus is telling the world, "I love the people you hate. I am willing to marry the people you dislike." He talks about himself as "living water" that always quenches our thirst and that he is the home everyone is seeking; and his love for the present is the way you get there. *The longest recorded conversation that Jesus had with any human being is the one he had with this Samaritan woman by the well.*

If we are to follow the Christ, the message is clear: we must give up the little world of our childhood hates and dislikes. Unlike old King David, who longed to go home to a smaller place and a simpler time, we must learn to find God right here, with us right now. We are always called to learn to love some of the people, places, and things we used to dislike out of our fears and ignorance.

I attended three great universities Furman, Harvard, and Vanderbilt. Each one was founded as a church-related school: one by the Baptists, one by the Pilgrims, and one by the Methodists. My liberal arts education gave me a tremendous foothold in life. The professors, experiences, and people in those three places taught me at a young age to learn how to love people and things I used to be ignorant about. That's what an education *should* do. I learned to love people of color at a time that our nation allowed racial segregation. My father was relatively poor, so I wanted and loved money. I planned to major in business and make a lot of it. But I wound up majoring in history and religion and being a preacher and a university chaplain.

I feared non-Christians, yet I emerged from college and went to graduate school in a place that had the only center for the study of world religions in the country. I was suspicious of scholars, and I revered athletes as "real men." I wound up working among scholars and teaching in a university.

I had no appreciation for classical music. Now my dearest and oldest close friend in life is the Dean of the Yale School of Music. I came from a fundamentalist religious background and emerged from my studies realizing that the truth of God is greater and more elusive than any one religion's ability to state it.

This is what following Jesus does to us. Jesus forces us to love that which we had previously not understood. Jesus is living water that keeps us from ever being thirsty again. The old prejudices are gone. We become married to something new. I still have many things I do not understand. We all do.

But I have learned that if ever I am to appreciate and taste the sweet, sweet, water of home, I must have a clean and forgiving heart.

Clean And Forgiving Hearts

—— the lessons ——

Do not remember the former things, or consider the things of old.

—Isaiah 43:18

Remember this and consider, recall it to mind, you transgressors,

—Isaiah 46:8

The angel of God who was going before the Israelite army moved and went behind them; and the pillar of cloud moved from in front of them and took its place behind them. It came between the army of Egypt and the army of Israel. And so the cloud was there with the darkness, and it lit up the night; one did not come near the other all night.

—Exodus 14:19-20

In the South Carolina town where I first ministered, most of the churches were named after theological terms or after Jesus' disciples. We had Saint Mark United Methodist Church, Trinity Baptist Church and Holy Trinity Episcopal Church. A historical church out in the country was different. It was named Return Baptist Church. Curiously, I asked one of their older members to tell me why the church had such an unusual name. The gentleman proceeded to tell me an amazing history. Many of the members of the original church 100 years earlier had been closely related family members. But in late 1890's, they had a big disagreement. The shouting and hard feelings went on for a few years. Eventually, half the membership left and moved down the road two miles to build another church they named Calvary Baptist Church.

The two churches existed apart from each other for 51 years, according to my source. Finally, in the 1940's, it dawned on some of the descendants in both churches that all those involved in the original fight had died, and people were having a hard time remembering the exact details of what it was their ancestors had fought about. Consequently, those in the newer church decided to sell their buildings and go back up the road two miles to the old church. To celebrate the event, they all decided to rename the original church,

"Return Baptist Church," in celebration of their family members and friends returning back up the road.

The past presents us with a paradox. A lot of *good things* happen to us. These things, if remembered, can give us great confidence in ourselves each day. Unfortunately, we sometimes forget those positive things that we should remember. On the other hand, some bad things happen to us in life. We can remember these bad things. They can become a lead weight, dragging us into despair.

The prophet Isaiah confronts the two-edged sword of memory in conflicting verses of Scripture. At one point, he begs his people to *remember* the former things of long ago. But at another point, he is just as adamant in demanding that his people *forget* the former things and not dwell on the past.

Remember and forget. Much of who we are as people and as nations revolves around how we edit our memories. Sometimes entire nations engage in selective memories. Consider the American Revolution. Our national consciousness remembers the determined colonial settler being pitted against foreign forces of the King of England. Actually, Americans fought Americans. Benjamin Franklin stopped speaking to his Tory son. Only a third of the colonists actively supported the war, and we are told by the historians that nearly as many Americans fought *for* Britain as fought *against* Britain.[8] Many scholars refer to the event as our first civil war.

Consider also some of our wonderful memories of Christopher Columbus. When he arrived in the New World, he frequently hanged 13 Indians at a time in honor of the 12 apostles and Jesus. Every male over 14 years of age had to bring a quota of gold every three months to the conquistadors. Those who could not pay this had their hands cut off "as a lesson." Half the 250,000 Indians on Haiti had been murdered or mutilated or had committed suicide within the first two years following Columbus' discovery of the New World.[9]

In recent years, a political party in Japan wanted to whitewash the Japanese history books and make Tojo a hero, in an effort to elect his daughter to governmental leadership.

Remember and forget. This is no small matter. It takes a clean and forgiving heart to learn from history and remember and own up to one's mistakes, as well as celebrate the right things in one's history. How timeless are the truths we find in the Bible about human life. There is an amazing event in the account of the Israelites' flight from Egypt. At one point, the Angel of God, which went before the Israelites as a cloud, had to turn around and stand behind them to help them close the door on their past. At that juncture, it was not so much the threat of the Red Sea in front of the people that created the panic, as it was the hosts of Egypt behind them. Harold Cooke Phillips is quite correct: *"Is it not true that often our greatest enemies are not those in front of us but those behind us?"*[10]

Many of us worry about the future. But is it not true that at our base level we, like the Israelites, are harassed not so much by the enemies we must one day meet as by the Egyptians we have already met? This is what makes life so difficult. At some point, we must set the Lord our God, not only before us, but behind us—between us and those memories from the past that would do us harm to accept as truth.

For this reason, following that one incident in the Bible, future scriptures about the exodus do not dwell upon the drowning of the Egyptian soldiers. Why dwell on that—they learned that after the angel of death passed over and murdered the Egyptian first-born, Pharaoh sent his soldiers after them anyway. In short, the murders accomplished nothing, so why pretend that they did? Violence against a people hardly ever makes them change their mind about the God you profess.

In this respect, Jesus' words have some healing power. His forgiving nature seems apparent in his teachings: "Love your enemies! If someone asks you to carry his pack one mile, you carry it two miles. Forgive people, 70 times seven. Parents, don't provoke your children to anger."

It is obvious that Jesus wants his followers to close the door to old hates so we can have a future. The parents of the Jivaro tribe of Indians in Ecuador have an amazing custom. Every night, when their children go to bed, they linger by their bedsides. They whisper into the ears of the children the names of all the people they must hate when they are older. This is the tribal way of keeping its feuds alive from generation to generation. And it has worked. Since 1599, when they slaughtered 25,000 outsiders who lived in two settlements, these savage headhunters still shrink the heads of enemies and remain unconquered. No outsiders go there. To be certain, the adults of the tribe have kept their hatred and negativity alive in the minds of their children for over 400 years.

Unfortunately, they have also kept savagery, illiteracy, and barbarism alive among their children.

Like an acid in the soul, or a bitter taste of rancid water in the mouth and throat, the constant remembrance of evil can eat away at each generation. Very precious things are ruined by keeping old grudges, resentments, and vexations in mind.

If we want to experience the sweet, sweet water of home, there are some things we have to forget. If we remember all the hurt we have experienced, life becomes clogged and choked. Life is essentially a process of managing our memories. We should constantly sort out our memories, throwing away things we ought to forget and keeping things that are precious. We either manage our memories, or they manage us.

Memories are in our lives to both warn us about evil and strengthen us about the possibilities for good. If we do not recast the memories we have of relationships with people who did us harm, we go through life, even if those people are long ago dead, forever seeking a chance to get even. Memories gallop into the present from the past.

A great power in life is to have our God move behind us and protect us from crippling memories. It is a truly adult and Christian experience to recast our past and maybe see now that love was there but was overshadowed by a misguided life or the demands of survival.

One of the amazing sagas of recorded history lies in the rela-tionship between Israel and Egypt. With the power of God standing behind her, Israel closed the door on the Egyptians chasing her. Whatever Israel was certain of at that time, one certainty was that the Egyptians were pagan, brutal, ruthless, and to be killed. After decades, some say centuries, of living in Egypt, including many years in servitude, they were freed. God had redeemed them from the Egyptians. That and the tears of suffering of their ancestors, they would never forget.

Yet as her future unfolded, Israel drew strength from an unusual source. In her battle with Assyria, her strongest ally was *Egypt*. In her battle with Babylon, her strongest ally was *Egypt*. When Nebu-chadnezzar had sacked the temple and slaughtered its priests, the prophet Jeremiah was rescued by *Egypt*. Even those examples pale in comparison to these shocking words from Matthew:

> *When they had gone, an angel of the Lord appeared to*
> *Joseph in a dream. "Get up," he said, "take the child and*
> *his mother and escape to Egypt. Stay there until I tell you,*
> *for Herod is going to search for the child to kill him."*

So he got up, took the child and his mother during the night and left for Egypt, where he stayed until the death of Herod.

What a marvelous "new thing" was this miracle as the Holy Family made its way toward Egypt. It totally transformed the cir-cumstances of heritage. That little family had to fully engage with its positive memories of some good people who remained in Egypt and leave behind the repressive memories of Herod and his brutal regime. They had to embrace and live with life's contradictions.

Our grandson was baptized in a little mountain church in the resort village of Blowing Rock, North Carolina. In reflecting on that event, I wondered what it would have been like to have had my deceased parents there at the service. That Sunday morning would have confused them. Both of them were born in 1908. My mother died in 1978, and my father died in 1985. Imagine the great conflicts of their adult world in America 1929-1978. In addition to the Great Depression, they faced wars in which they participated and feared their children would get drafted into. If suddenly they showed up in the Blowing Rock Methodist Church and saw me, their aging son, wearing a shirt made in Viet Nam, getting out of my car made in Japan, and hugging an opera singer from Germany while thanking her for singing the song we wanted sung at the baptism, what would they think?

The Bible is a book that helps people live with contradictions and conflicting memories they can't understand until clean and forgiving hearts can carry the day. I look at Israel and Egypt throughout the centuries, and I remain hopeful that the United States and our enemies of the present day will get together out there somewhere in the future. We have to have memories short enough to enable us to engage fully and hopefully with former enemies. We have to have memories long enough to discourage expansionism and blatant disregard for human rights. We have to live with that contradiction of forgetting some things and never forgetting other things.

Opposing authoritarianism and engaging with hope those who practice it is a contradiction we live with. It would be good to view some of our enemies as welcomed markets for our products and suppliers of many items we also need. We have to forget and overlook some history. But when nations makes vassals out of other nations and their own working class, repress religious expression, and arrest people for expressing a desire to be free, we should remember our own heritage of justice and freedom.

We remember, and we forget. With dignity and patience, we stand for freedom, but also with tenacity and no apologies we criticize repression until clean and loving hearts can emerge. We can learn a lot from Isaiah:

Do not remember the things of old—Remember the former things of old.

PART FOUR

— A Horse of a Different Color —

A Horse of a Different Color

— t h e   l e s s o n s —

"The harvest is past, the summer is ended, and we are not saved."
For the hurt of my poor people I am hurt, I mourn, and dismay has
taken hold of me. Is there no balm in Gilead? Is there no physician
there? Why then has the health of my poor people not been restored?

–Jeremiah 8:20-22

Then I saw the lamb open one of the seven seals, and I heard one of
the four living creatures call out, as with a voice of thunder, "Come!"
I looked, and there was a white horse! Its rider had a bow; a crown
was given to him, and he came out conquering and to conquer.

When he opened the second seal, I heard the second living creature
call out, "Come!" And out came another horse, bright red; its rider was
permitted to take peace from the earth, so that people would slaughter
one another; and he was given a great sword.

When he opened the third seal, I heard the third living creature call
out, "Come!" I looked, and there was a black horse! Its rider held a pair
of scales in his hand, and I heard what seemed to be a voice in the midst
of the four living creatures saying, "A quart of wheat for a day's pay, and
three quarts of barley for a day's pay, but do not damage the olive oil
and the wine!"

When he opened the fourth seal, I heard the voice of the fourth living
creature call out, "Come!" I looked and there was a pale green horse! Its
rider's name was Death, and Hades followed with him; they were given
authority over a fourth of the earth, to kill with sword, famine,
and pestilence, and by the wild animals of the earth.

–Revelation 6:1-8

The past, the present, and the future often come together in America every 4th of July, as we observe our national Independence Day. According to our Scriptures, the past, present, and future are often represented by Faith, Hope, and Love. Faith represents the past to a great degree; we have faith in something because we have experienced it or been told about it by someone. Love, on the other hand, has to take place in the present in order to be genuine. To say you loved your spouse the first year of your marriage amounts to little now. Hope, however, has to do with our attitudes about the future.

We have a lot of faith in our country's past actions. People tell us great stories about the past, from the rockets' red glare and the bombs bursting in air of Francis Scott Key; to the land of the free, epitomized by Ellis Island and the Statue of Liberty; and to the home of the brave, defended by our greatest generation in World War II. Likewise, we all have a lot of love for our country today as rightfully expressed by our stirring patriotic music and our parades. We have faith in our country, and we love it. What about hope for our country's future? What about hope?

I believe our country is like parents walking with a little girl. You've probably done it yourself. The little girl is in the middle with each parent holding one of her hands. As they stroll, the parents will periodically count one, two, three, and swing her up in the air. The little girl just squeals in delight, and together the family makes its way slowly down the sidewalk. If you consider that image, you begin to realize that no matter how strong are the parents, the entire procession is controlled by the child. The speed at which the family moves is dependent on how fast or slow the little girl is moving. That is how it is with faith, love, and hope. We spend a lot of time in the church talking about the big two, faith and love. But faith and love do not travel very far or very fast without hope. Without hope for a meaningful future for our nation, it is hard to get people energized, regardless of our past history and our present love for our country.

For much of my mother's life, her earthly hope was the James Walker Memorial Hospital in Wilmington, North Carolina. She carried around in her purse a black and white photo of that hospital. My mother had had two infants, my sister and my brother, die within hours of their births. Doctors offered no hope she would be able to safely deliver a healthy baby. But immediately following World War II, a new medical procedure called a Caesarean section began to be offered in a few select hospitals. The James Walker Memorial Hospital was one of those few. So her earthly medical hope became a reality.

The prophet Jeremiah raised questions about earthly hope with his people. "The harvest is past, the summer is ended, and we are not saved." The prophet cried, "Is there no balm in Gilead? Is there no physician there? Why, is there no healing for the wounds of my people?"

In Jeremiah's world, Gilead was the medical center. It was the ancient equivalent of the Mayo Clinic. Gilead was a center of hope. The doctors at Gilead extracted remedies from the herbs, flowers, and trees, which grew only in that area. The balm referred to by Jeremiah was a popular medicine made from the resin of a tree that grew in Gilead.[1] Many an ancient Jew said to his or her children, "If I get really sick, get me to Gilead!" Suddenly, a change took place in that world. Jeremiah saw his nation as sick and dependent on inadequate remedies. The people believed that just time and prayer would cure the ills of the nation and bring peace and security again. But they needed more than just time and prayer.

Jeremiah looked at his world, and he saw what we can see: war, famine, disease, and death. His questions are good ones; where are the remedies? Are there no medicines, no physicians, and no governments that can stop this mess? Jeremiah raised a great issue: With all the power we have, why is there no easy healing for the wounds of our people?

Some of the most vivid images of devastation are those of John of Patmos. John figuratively depicts four horsemen who ride among humans. The four horsemen are dressed in white, red, black, and pale. They stand for war, famine, disease, and death. The four horsemen are not some people who are going to appear at a certain moment in history. They are already here.

The one dressed in white is the announcer, the conqueror, wielding an archer's bow with arrows. The bow and arrow is not a noisy weapon, like bombs and rifles. His arrows represent the silent poison of greed. He streaks through financial institutions. His victims have to sell their heritage and their land and watch themselves and their family members lose jobs and security.

Next, the one dressed in red speaks. "My way is the easiest way," he continues. "A little mistrust here, some bruised egos there, a little accident maybe, and they will break out their weapons. They will slaughter each other. It's easy to take away peace from the earth. When they get frustrated, angry, and fearful, the humans will reason, 'War is best.'"

The rider of the black horse disagrees. "War and economic disasters are loud and messy things. They are also very expensive. Hunger is better. With war you get arrogant people who think they have won. But with famine, the hungry will just suffer quietly and die."

Finally, the rider of the pale horse speaks. He is called disease and death. He speaks, "My way is better still. War and famine are selective. Leaders survive wars, and the wealthy can survive famine. My methods are certain. AIDS and cancer are the swords I wield today."[2]

Who is safe from these powers? Where on this earth is our final hope? Why is there no healing for war, famine, disease, and death? There is a beautiful scene in the movie and book called the Wizard of Oz. During a welcome departure from their tough journey along the yellow brick road and across the field of poppies, Dorothy and Toto, the Scarecrow, the Tin Woodsman, and the Lion are driven about in a coach. The coach is drawn by a magical colored horse. As they ride around and around Emerald City's fountain in the square, the horse changes color. It changes from emerald green to royal purple. Then it becomes yellow and brilliant orange right before their delighted eyes. The riders ask the coachman what kind of horse it is. He laughs and responds: "Why that's the horse of a different color." Then the group passes the day away singing and laughing in the Land of Oz.[3]

The horse of a different color appears to be our ultimate hope in a world of greed, war, famine, and disease. Out of the depths of our frustration, we sometimes see evil influences in life and, like Jeremiah, cry out that life is not good but evil; that some demon monsters are in control of the lives of humans—it's nothing but the survival of the fittest and every person for himself or herself. One of the amazing things to come out of the spiritual dilemma of slavery in America is a horse of a different color called the Negro Spiritual. The existence of these songs is a monument to a people who forged hope out of shackles. The slaves found something universal about life itself. They pointed to a horse of a different color. Armed with their assurance that God is the ultimate hope in life, they straightened the question mark in Jeremiah's sentence into an exclamation point: There *is* a balm in Gilead! To make the spirit whole. There *is* a balm in Gilead! To heal the sin-sick soul.

Jesus the Christ, himself, was a horse of a different color on the world's religious scene. He was a messiah, but he also suffered. He was a poor carpenter, but he became the victor over life and death. He was one who took the cheap seats at every banquet, but he sits at the right hand of God the Father. He was one who favored justice over status, fairness over comfort, and tolerance over smugness. He was different.

The United States of America, in spite of all its faults, was a horse of a different color. It practiced thrift instead of spending, embraced manufacturing instead of abject consumerism, rebuilt the nations it had conquered instead of destroying them, marched toward justice for all of its citizens, effected rule by law instead of by religion, and provided opportunity for all instead of for a select few self-interested people. It did not adopt the techniques of its enemies, but held itself to higher ethical standards in warfare than did its enemies. The poor, tired, and sick masses the world over said, "There is a balm in America. If I get my back to the wall, get me to America." We were a horse of a different color. And I think we still are. I think it will be slow and agonizing, but I believe this generation will make it. They may have to live with less and retrain and go hungry at times. But I am greatly encouraged. Show me an example, someone might ask.

A major article titled "Forswearing Greed" was published in *The Economist* (June 2009), a major European business magazine. It chronicled how one graduating MBA student, just three weeks before the graduation of his class at Harvard Business School, circulated an oath for managers and asked any members of the graduating class who felt the same way to show up for an unofficial ceremony on the day before they received their MBA degrees. Of the 800 in the graduating class, over 400 showed up. They all swore the following: "I promise to serve the greater good, act with the utmost integrity, and guard against decisions and behavior that advance my own narrow ambitions but harm the enterprise and the societies it serves."

When asked afterward why they did this, the students said they wanted to distance themselves from earlier generations whose "wonky moral compasses have contributed to the present turmoil." Defenders of the oath claim that only working to maximize shareholder value has become a justification for short-termism and rapid personal gain. Now, we can snicker at the naiveté of these students. Many of them may not get jobs anyway. A number will go into non-profit and government jobs in the bad economic climate, so embracing values could prove useful. And most CEO's don't get MBA's anyway.

But they are, by their effort, a horse of a different color from their professors who tend to swallow Milton Friedman's claim that the only responsibility of business is to maximize profits. And there is something about our American heritage that produces such things. If you can prove me different, I will defer and retract. This is America, this is still America where trust in God, and in the belief in the dignity and worth of the human being as more than an economic creature, has held sway. Show me a leading business school in China or Japan or Europe or anywhere where over half the graduating class would, on their own, swear allegiance to such an oath, especially in troubled times. We are a horse of a different color. That inheritance from our past is our hope for recovering peace of mind as a society. It means that we must retain that inheritance, not sell it, live up to its high calling and find an appropriate guidance system to help us carry it through turbulent times as a society.

Don't Sell What You Don't Own

—— *the lessons* ——

Those who are unspiritual do not receive the gifts of God's spirit, for they are foolishness to them, and they are unable to understand them because they are spiritually discerned. Those who are spiritual discern all things, and they are themselves subject to no one else's scrutiny. "For who has known the mind of the Lord so as to instruct him?" But we have the mind of Christ.

—*1 Corinthians 2:14-16*

I appeal to you therefore, brothers and sisters, by the mercies of God, to present your bodies as a living sacrifice, holy and acceptable to God, which is your spiritual worship. Do not be conformed to this world, but be transformed by the renewing of your minds, so that you may discern what is the will of God—what is good and acceptable and perfect.

—*Romans 12:1-2*

W hen I was a boy, a marvelous man named Major Rhymes lived in the house behind ours. Major Rhymes was an officer in the U.S. Army and was stationed at Fort Gordon in Augusta. He always let us children play with his military equipment. We could camp out in the backyard with all manner of tents, canteens, knives, shovels, and helmets.

One week, a crisis developed. I was marching around the neighborhood with Major Rhymes' helmet on my head. One of my friends, Buddy Lewis, offered to buy the helmet from me for $3.00. So I sold it to him. A few days later, Major Rhymes was called to direct some infantry maneuvers, and he came to our house to get his helmet back. I'll never forget the constant voice of my mother, "You can't sell what you don't own."

"You can't sell what you don't own." That's a hard message for humans to accept. From the time of Adam and Eve down to the present day, some humans tend to think Darwin was wrong. They appear to think, "It's really not survival of the fittest; it's survival of the slickest."

The evidence is there in most of the history of our own country—from the very beginning. In the year 1626, a politician in Amsterdam wrote a letter to the legislative assembly of The Netherlands. He described the people of New Netherland and casually wrote that they had purchased the island of Manhattan from the savages for the value of 60 guilders—about 24 dollars worth of beads and trinkets.

In grammar school, we learned about that real estate deal. We heard it told as the Great Manhattan Swindle. Peter Minuit made the deal to legally purchase the island from the Indians at a dollar a square mile. There was even an ornate document to seal the deal. Historians are fond of computing the rate of appreciation and telling us what a great swindle it was.[4] And it was a swindle. The early European colonists rarely reimbursed the Indians at all for the lands they took. The purchasing power of the dollar in 1626 was such that in a modern equivalent, the Dutch paid many hundreds of thousands of dollars for Manhattan. It was a scam. The Dutch purchased the island from the Canarsie Indians. Only later did they find out that the Canarsie Indians did not live on Manhattan Island. They were only there visiting some other Indians.

The Carnasie Indians sold something they never owned in the first place. After they ripped off supposedly one of the world's smartest real estate dealers, they got in their canoes and returned home, across the river to Brooklyn, where they actually lived.[5] It was quite a swindle. Mother was right. "You should never sell what you don't own." And you should never buy something from someone that *they* don't own. I kept Buddy Lewis' three dollars even after Major Rhymes got his helmet back.

I begin this way because I firmly believe that much of our confusion and loneliness in life comes because sometimes we as individuals, as churches, and even as societies sell precious values that we do not own. Sometimes in our effort to make God very popular and approachable in a modern world, we get scammed. If, out of ignorance, we sell the legacy of our faith, we do ourselves and others serious harm.

We have sometimes found that it is possible to be psychologically well and ethically sick. The search for personal peace of mind is not the highest goal in life. People can get their lives together at very low ethical levels. Some churches have even bought a corporate image of worship and programming, where telecommunications and megatrends in society seem to replace theology. It is my belief that Christianity should enhance, not compromise human dignity. Markets serve those who pay, but Christianity steps in to help those who cannot pay. Politics is about the balance of power, but Christianity steps in to help those who have no power. Economic systems create problems that cannot be resolved by economics alone. We must also have the impetus of faith, hope, and love that our faith calls upon us to show toward God and toward our neighbors.

Many hundreds of years ago, the apostle Paul wrote letters to the churches at Corinth and Rome. He wrote to sophisticated, liberated people who were in the process of selling something they didn't own—their dignity as moral, righteous creatures of God. Paul laid out two kinds of wisdom—Christian wisdom and worldly wisdom. He talked about how human wisdom must always serve some higher purpose beyond itself. Paul had a high view of human dignity. He asserted that since Christ has become one with us, through his death to redeem us, whatever we link our bodies, minds, and ethics to links Christ to those same things.

We must never sell the moral and ethical demands of Christ, regardless of how slick that might make us appear in a modern world. Affirming the dignity and worth of human beings is not ours to sell. If we treat people as objects, simply as financial capital, we stand as an affront to the God who claims we should love our neighbor as we do ourselves. Hopefully, we will not totally sell off to foreign countries the jobs that provide a livelihood for our workers so one percent of our population can benefit. Are we selling away people whom we do not own?

Is that not the message in the parables when Jesus told about

a man who buried a talent in the ground, when he talked about
foolish and unprepared maidens who missed the coming of the
bridegroom, and when he responded to the lawyer who asked him,
"Who is my neighbor?"

Thanks to the visionary thinking of its board of directors and
worshippers, the seasonal church that I pastor in summer months
was saved from annihilation a few years ago. A feasibility study for
the Blowing Rock Methodist Church was compiled by the parent
denomination, claiming that since this church had few facilities,
it could not possibly succeed as a church. It recommended that
the church move into a facility being vacated at that time by
another church.

The report concluded that if the church stayed in its present
location, its only recourse would be to "seek to minister to visitors
and vacationers through a Saturday night worship service, which
might be more contemporary in style." In the face of this report,
and a subsequent eviction notice by the trustees of the Methodist Foundation, members of the church board decided that the
102-year-old heritage of the church was not theirs to sell out on. The
current generation does not own the 102 years of prayer, struggle,
and worship that took place there. So they would not abandon the
legacy of the little church. They would not sell what they did not
own. They boldly reached out and bought the premises to keep the
rich heritage that had been given the old, simple church by God
and by countless dedicated people from far and near. And that
spirit opened up a flood-gate for Methodists, Baptists, Episcopa-
lians, Presbyterians, Catholics, Lutherans, and nondenominational
worshippers to come there and add their names to the great spirit
of an old and simple place, a spirit that none of us owns or has a
right to sell.

The church, over the past decade, remains a place that overflows
with several hundred worshippers each Sunday and donates over
$50,000 in unrestricted benevolence offering to the community's

social agencies each season. All this is done despite the fact that the church is only open four months a year, has no telephone, has no parking spaces, and has no budget.

It's amazing how we humans, through a lack of understanding, sell out some old and simple religious things that could have so much meaning for us if we but understood their purpose and history. I can remember a lesson about a simple prayer that most of us know. The prayer goes:

> *Now I lay me down to sleep;*
> *I pray the Lord my soul to keep.*
> *If I should die before I wake,*
> *I pray the Lord my soul to take.*

I once heard a young mother say that her child was using that simple little prayer *now*, but she hoped that when he grew older, he would discard it for something better, more contemporary, and more meaningful. I responded: "You want something more meaningful than that?" I asked her to do some research into the story of John Rogers, the author of that simple prayer, and directed her to the Houghton Library at Harvard to look at the New England Primer.

The New England Primer was the universal text for children in New England and the East. First printed in 1689, over six million copies were in existence to help children learn their alphabet and learn how to read. But very few remain in existence now—they are very rare. The Houghton Library has three copies. One belonged to Nathaniel Hawthorne; another belonged to the family of Emily Dickinson; the third belonged to Herman Melville, the author of *Moby Dick*.

When you open the Primer, the alphabet appears first. Immediately after the alphabet appears, "Now I lay me down to sleep." The Primer also features Puritan John Rogers' "Exultation to His Children" as he was about to be burned at the stake. That is followed by a woodcut illustration of John Rogers actually burning at the stake surrounded by his wife and nine children, with his tenth child, an infant, being held by his wife. It was because of his teaching Protestant doctrine in England that John Rogers was burned to death; and knowing that could happen, he taught his family the little prayer.

A few years later, I had occasion to encounter this same mother on another trip to New England. She reported that the simple little prayer, "Now I lay me down to sleep," was no longer being said just by her child. The whole family was saying it every night. She was so excited just knowing that each evening she could communicate over the centuries with something that was so precious to such a great man as John Rogers. The prayer has not changed; its words are the same as before. She has changed. She has just not sold something that was not hers to sell anyway. We should never sell what we do not own.

Living Up To Our Nametag

—— *the   lesson* ——

Now when Jesus came into the district of Caesarea Philippi, he asked his disciples, "Who do people say that the Son of Man is?" And they said, "Some say John the Baptist, but others Elijah, and still others Jeremiah or one of the prophets." He said to them, "But who do you say that I am?" Simon Peter answered, "You are the Messiah, the Son of the living God."

–Matthew 16:13-20

Wherever we go in America, we confront the nametag. At service clubs, a nametag is as important as a vigorous handshake or a congenial welcome. Public relations experts refer to uniformity of name tags as important in "branding" an organization.

One fall, I was on a panel at a conference being held at Hilton Head Island. Another panel member was Dr. Jack McConnell. Jack had retired to the beach after an illustrious biomedical research career. He was one of the inventors of the tuberculosis test and the MRI, and he was the primary inventor of Tylenol.

Jack tried to be "what they call a typical retiree: play golf, eat at restaurants, and travel." That's why he went to Hilton Head. But 12,000 working poor also live in Hilton Head, and Jack noticed them. Many did not have health insurance or access to care. He wondered what could be done about it. Then, he found the answer in himself. "It wasn't until I stopped saying, 'Someone should look into this problem' and realized that I was speaking to myself that it really turned around," McConnell said. In 1994, Jack founded the Volunteers in Medicine free clinic, staffed by retired doctors, retired nurses, retired dentists, and retired lay people, all volunteers. Obtaining South Carolina licenses for retired physicians from other states and finding a way to pay for malpractice insurance were two major hurdles he overcame. That one clinic has had over 150,000 patient visits, and 63 clinics just like it have opened in 22 states across the United States. North Carolina has the largest number of clinics—11.

The conference at which Jack and I were presenting gave us a huge nametag that had our first name in enormous letters and the last name just under it in very small type. For example, mine had "Hal" in letters four inches high, and the "Warlick" was so small you could hardly see it. The organizers of the conference wanted to create a casual, friendly atmosphere. One day the previous year, the conference had a two hour lunch break. Jack was tired so he went outside and sat on one of the benches beside the number one tee of the Harbor Town golf course to soak up some sun. He was by himself and had been there in a drowsy but peaceful mood for about 30 minutes. He was sitting there with his eyes closed, enjoying the sunshine on his face and the birds singing when two women drove up in a golf cart to play golf.

When they got out of their cart to tee off, one of them said, "Look at that old man over there asleep. Why has he got that big nametag with 'Jack' on it?" The other woman confidently said, "I know exactly why he must have that nametag. That poor fellow obviously has dementia. His caregivers have placed it around his neck so if he gets lost he can read it and tell people who he is!"

The two golfers certainly misread Jack's identity and purpose. But this issue is an important one; what is the nametag we have to live up to, as people and as a country? Jesus himself raised the central question, "Who do people say I am?" He, too, wanted to find out the nametag other people, especially strangers, were assigning to him. In Caesarea Philippi, Jesus confronted his disciples with questions that were troubling him. He asked, "How does the world view me? What nametag do people put on me?" They responded, "Oh, some say you're like the other prophets, another Elijah or

Jeremiah. Others say you are a great preacher and maverick like John the Baptist."

That didn't satisfy Jesus. So he asked the question another way: "Well, who do you say that I am? You are my friends. What nametag do you place on me and want me to wear?" Finally, Peter answered, "You are the Christ, the Son of the living God." Jesus was more pleased with that answer. But it still wasn't enough.

Later, when he told the disciples that his nametag required him to suffer, Peter rebuked him and tried to get in his way. So Jesus took Peter, James, and John and drew away from the crowds to retreat into the mountains. There, he put the question a third way: "Who does God say that I am? What nametag has God placed on me?" It was at that point that Jesus set his face to go to Jerusalem to give up his life. The disciples then knew just how lofty a nametag Jesus was wearing and if they were going to try to live up to the nametag of following him, it wasn't going to be easy. They had to identify higher than mere humans.

Some people, like Jack McConnell, live far above the nametag that two passing strangers would put on them. And other people have listened to their own publicity so much they haven't even begun to touch in reality the image they project in their public branding of themselves. It's also true of nations. Who are we as Americans? How do other people see us? How do we see ourselves, especially when we celebrate our nation's independence?

We are seen, obviously, by much of the world as affluent in resources and heritage. What is the nametag we have to live up to? Here it gets tricky and more difficult. The place, perhaps, to begin is with the word "freedom." We certainly wear that on our nametag. No other country puts as much emphasis on freedom as the United States of America. Our national anthem calls us the "land of the free." From Abraham Lincoln, to Susan B. Anthony, to Martin Luther King, Americans have been urged to live up to their nametag of "freedom." When a group of French politicians wanted to flatter the United States, they sent the Statue of Liberty. No other country boasts as much about its desire to bring liberty to the rest of the world. Just how good are we at living up to that nametag?

Some nations look at us, and they point out that we have one of the highest rates of imprisonment in the world and that prison building is one of our biggest growth industries. In fact, we have two million children who have a parent in prison. In some ways, we may not live up to our nametag. But those same nations recognize what is, perhaps, the most admirable trait we have. Even as we dredge through depressing statistics, Europeans recognize, and I quote them, "that the American system has proved to be admirably self-correcting."[6]

This is the key to our nametag. We embrace freedom, and we self-correct. When we mess up in civil liberties, we correct in a swift and dogged manner. Congress has reined in warrantless wiretapping. The press leaks material. The courts have sometimes been slow, but the Supreme Court has forced us to extend the Geneva Convention's articles to inmates in military prisons and especially in Guantanamo. You read the foreign newspapers and magazines, and you realize that they see this. In fact, they are most impressed by one thing in our political process—in our last presidential race, the three prime candidates for president, Hillary Clinton, John McCain, and Barack Obama, all condemned torture and illegal detention and declared publicly and vociferously their desire to close Guantanamo.

That would not happen in any other country in the world. We Americans try to self correct when it comes to issues of freedom. These candidates disagreed on the economy, on heathcare, on the problems in the Middle East, and on social security, but on one thing they were united: no person in this country need go to bed and worry that he or she will be illegally arrested and be without representation and human rights.

My Bible is 1,051 pages long, largely because it self-corrects. It has two creation stories because it self-corrects. It has at least four perspectives on Israelite history. These offer different perspectives on the same historical events, with each perspective becoming more compassionate and just than the previous one. It has four gospels and 66 books. Ecclesiastes is a self-correction on some of the shallowness of the Proverbs. And look at some of the characters in the Bible. With God's help, Jacob self-corrects his situation with Esau. Joseph self-corrects his arrogance toward his brothers. Moses, with a price on his head, self-corrects his murderous temperament and returns to the scene of his crime, Egypt, and gets it right the second time. Paul self-corrects his hatred of the followers of Jesus and becomes their champion. That is what God does for us—God gives us the power of self correction. When we fall down, we can get up and get it right.

We should never take that for granted. Japan, for example, is hard on welfare recipients. Unable to by food, three men died in one Japanese city last year. They just wasted away. To the Japanese government, those in need are not citizens. Only those who pay taxes are citizens. With no tradition of charity, Japan has few food kitchens or places for the indigent. Those that are there are run by Christian missionaries from South Korea or Japan's tiny Christian population. Those are the words of the *New York Times*, not my words.

In the Unites States, we have a big problem with the homeless on the streets. Over half the Black males in the inner cities drop out of school before graduating. We fall down. But we get up. With God's help, we try to self-correct. Over a third of the institutions that provide social welfare in America's big cities are religious. One British writer commented, "(In America), people of faith do a disproportionate share of the heavy lifting when it comes to dealing with exclusion. These are the people who man the soup kitchens and look after the children of prisoners."[7] We fall down, but with God's help, we self-correct.

— t h e   l e s s o n s —

When I was a child, I spoke like a child, I thought like a child, I reasoned like a child; when I became an adult, I put an end to childish ways.

–1 Corinthians 13:11

Then his mother and his brothers came; and standing outside, they sent to him and called him. A crowd was sitting around him; and they said to him, "Your mother and your brothers and sisters are outside, asking for you." And he replied, "Who are my mother and my brothers?" And looking at those who sat around him, he said, "Here are my mother and my brothers!"

–Mark 3:31-34

I spent an afternoon conducting a brief survey. I called some college students and asked them if they know what a Tom-Tom is. Eighty percent of them correctly identified a Tom-Tom as a Global Positioning System that goes in a car. Tom-Tom is called the world's leading navigation solutions provider. Since 15 percent of all highways and roads change each year, a GPS helps everyone, from babysitters rushing to get to an unfamiliar house to college students stuck in traffic coming from a mall, find a back way to where they are going. Having correct directions is important in many avenues of life.

You and I live our *inner lives* according to the directions we have drawn for ourselves in terms of what the ever-changing world is really like. We began acquiring and mapping these directions when we were little children. Sometimes when we are adults, we find ourselves still trying to operate with the directional systems we installed for ourselves when we were small children. Consequently, we can go through life not truly understanding the reality of the adult world we live in, much less the reality of God's goodness. Psychologists have a definition for people who try to live in their adult world with the directional systems they formed as children. The definition is *transference*. It is a way of seeing the world through a guidance system that was developed in childhood and was entirely appropriate to childhood, but which is inappropriately transferred into adult situations. The apostle Paul spoke vividly of the acceptance of reality when he told the Corinthians: "When I was a child, I spoke like a child, I thought like a child, I reasoned like a child; when I became an adult, I gave up childish ways . . ." (1 Corinthians 13:11).

Let me illustrate this phenomenon. Parents, at times, unconsciously disappoint children. Perhaps they promise a trip for a birthday and then forget about it and give a sweater instead. It happens to all of us. But if it happens too often and disappointment follows disappointment, the child sees a lack of caring and learns not to trust. Then, in his childish way, he forms his map of reality on the basis of this repeated experience. *It diminishes a person's pain to believe other persons are basically untrustworthy*; that way they don't have to expect *anything*. If promises are not kept over and over, someone can conclude, "I just can't trust anybody."

When we do not bother to reprogram our internal guidance system to see if other people are truly untrustworthy, we tend to expect the worst in life. We can become angry with life and quarrel with it on the basis of positions drawn when we were little boys or little girls. When I was in college, my best friend from childhood received a birthday gift every year on December 18th from his aunt in Hattiesburg, Mississippi. He hadn't seen her in years. The gift was always for a 12-year-old boy. My friend would laugh and say, "Aunt Grace still thinks of me as a little boy."

When he was just seven years old, I took my oldest son to a store in Massachusetts to buy him his very first baseball glove. I let him pick it out, and we made a big deal over it. We even pitched ball in the aisle to make certain it was the right one. Maybe he remembers it, and maybe he doesn't. But for years, I had remembered how I got *my* first baseball glove. When I was a child, many stores gave trading stamps to the customers based on the dollar amounts purchased. You pasted these S & H Green Stamps or Top Value stamps in little coupon books. Then you could go to a stamp redemption center and trade your books of stamps for prizes. It seemed like it took forever to fill up the books. You could trade 10 books for a toaster. Of course, you had to purchase groceries for a year at that store to get enough for the toaster. But many homemakers were into that. And occasionally, you could get something after a few years of stamp collecting that you didn't have the extra money to purchase.

On my 13th birthday, I walked into our house after school let out for the day. I had asked for a baseball glove for months. Mother couldn't be home, so she left my present on the kitchen table. There it was, in a brown S & H Green Stamp bag—a baseball glove. It was to my mind a horrible glove. It was the most pitiful looking glove I had ever seen. My folks knew nothing about baseball. It was too small. It was inflexible. It was cheaply made. I never used it a single time. I told my mother I did not like it. I wound up purchasing a used glove from a friend. After many months, I threw the Green Stamp glove in the trash, still brand new and never used.

From that and several other legitimate experiences, I carried certain memories into a road map for life for a long time—my parents were poor, uninformed, and very much people who had to struggle against life. I had the road map of a victim. It angered me.

Many years later, immediately before the funeral service for my mother, one of my hometown friends walked over. He said, "Warlick, you certainly were lucky. Your mother had a wonderful life and was so privileged in many ways." I responded, "Are you kidding me? She had to struggle like crazy. My first baseball glove came from Green Stamps, my father went bankrupt when the textile mill closed, and we had to move here and buy a house half the size of the one we lived in." He quickly answered, "No, that's not what I meant. Look over at the casket at all the guys your mother taught and influenced in Sunday School and Cub Scouts. Not many women have ever helped teach successful people like them."

I started developing a new guidance system. I remembered that on the day of my first baseball glove, Mother had been at an all-day teacher's workshop at the church. And during the year of the Green Stamps glove, our church had built a new building for a mission church, and my father had done much of the electrical work for it at no charge to the church. *My parents got the glove wrong, but they got life right.* Gloves are important to children; so are a lot of other toys, unfortunately, much moreso than values. But adults ought to know better. Adults should redraw their maps of life through the practical wisdom of adult eyes. I tell the college students to whom I preach that college is a time for students to start developing better guidance systems. If not, they will *always get the toys right but get life wrong.* Aristotle made the claim that good people possess *phronesis*, or practical wisdom. Practical wisdom is making appropriate adjustments in our preconceived categories so that our behavior fits the specific situation.

One day, when His mother and brothers came seeking Him, Jesus left them standing long enough to say this to His followers: "My real mother and brothers and sisters are those who do the will of God." Jesus was not rejecting His family. Nor was He rejecting family values. He was simply drawing a new map of reality. He was insisting that there is a reality beyond the earthly family, an allegiance beside which even family ties must take second place. There is an even greater family to which we belong. Being baptized by the Holy Spirit into the Kingdom of God causes you to understand the need to always reassess your directions in the light of God's grace. We have to base our guidance systems on the family of God to which we belong, *one* family of God. "By his spirit," says Paul, we travel in a new direction. "We are all baptized into one body—Jew or Greek, slave or free, male or female, rich or poor, teacher or students— all were made to drink of one Spirit." In baptism, we are stamped as the property of God. This gives us a bond with one another that turns life in another direction. We are supposed to journey with a better guidance system than our childhood wants and expressions can offer us as adults.

Many people can quote the morbid negative social and economic indicators. Greed, ignorance, and white collar crime seem to have reached new heights. The economic system is in the tank as I write this, and we have many significant problems in our America. Too many people have focused on getting the toys right and have gotten life wrong. But we should not fall into that trap ever again. Life is not about toys.

Many people are making sacrifices so students in this country can get a college education. The best industry in the United States is higher education. International rankings show that 80 percent of the best universities in the world are in the United States. Our nation has just five percent of the world's population, yet 21 of the world's top 50 universities are in our country. It is astonishing that 2.6 percent of America's Gross Domestic Product goes to higher education, compared to second place Europe's 1.1 percent, less than half what we place into it. We Americans put eight times the percentage of our economy into our colleges and universities than does the average for the rest of the world. We do not do that so students will be able to buy more toys as adults. We do it so we can stay a democracy. We stand at a critical juncture in our country. We can recover from the housing and mortgage debacle, the bank messes, and the stock failures. It may take much longer than people realize. But illiteracy in our country is growing, and that threatens the very fabric of our country.

Thomas Jefferson said it best, "If a nation expects to be ignorant *and free* . . . it expects what never was and what never will be." I pray that all of us will use our time and energy to trust God to help us reprogram some of our guidance systems. The life of Jesus redrew the world's map as to religion's need to reach out to people and to tell the truth, that we should love God with our bodies, our minds, and our souls—and that we should love our neighbor as we love ourselves.

We have had our bailouts. As Christians, we owe the Lord who saved us our best efforts at life. We owe our Lord more than a handful of parties attended, a sack full of toys accumulated, and a perpetual ignorance. "When I was a child, I spoke like a child, I got bored like a child, I revolved everything around myself—when I became an adult, I realized I needed a new guidance system."

What's in it for Others?

— the lesson —

Someone in the crowd said to him, "Teacher, tell my brother to divide the family inheritance with me." But he said to him, "Friend, who set me to be a judge or arbitrator over you?" And he said to them, "Take care! Be on your guard against all kinds of greed; for one's life does not consist in the abundance of possessions." Then he told them a parable: "The land of a rich man produced abundantly. And he thought to himself, 'What should I do, for I have no place to store my crops?' Then he said, 'I will do this: I will pull down my barns and build larger ones, and there I will store all my grain and my goods. And I will say to my soul, Soul you have ample goods laid up for many years; relax, eat, drink, be merry.' But God said to him, 'You fool! This very night your life is being demanded of you. And the things you have prepared, whose will they be?' So it is with those who store up treasures for themselves but are not rich toward God."

He said to his disciples, "Therefore I tell you, do not worry about your life, what you will eat, or about your body, what you will wear. For life is more than food and the body more than clothing.

–Luke 12:13-23

My senior year of high school was supposed to be one of the grandest athletic years in my life. It wasn't. Our football team returned 17 starters from a squad that had won 10 of 11 games, and had been ranked number one in the state the previous year. That senior year for us was to be a cake walk through the competition. It was not. We were bigger, faster, and more experienced, but we barely had a winning record. No one could understand it.

We had a certain player on the team that I will call David. It was only several years later, when I was in college, that I learned that we had played the whole season under what I now call "David's Rules of Acquisition." Unknown to the rest of us on the team, David's father gave him today's equivalent of $100 every time he scored a touchdown. Whenever we were near the other team's goal line, I remember that David always jumped around in the huddle wanting the ball.

One Christmas at a high school reunion, a few of us went over to the home of our old high school coach and looked at a few films of our games. It didn't take long to see what we had feared: If David didn't get to run with the ball, he didn't block for anyone else to run. David's rule of acquisition was, "What's in it for me?"

We Christians have to deal with Jesus' Rules of Acquisition. They're quite different, indeed. The Scripture lesson is quite clear. "Be on guard against greed . . . one's life does not consist of posses-sions . . . life is more than food and the body more than clothing . . . where your treasure is, there your heart will be also." That's a pretty radical perspective, for most of us.

John Wesley, the founder of the Methodist movement, said that no Methodist could wear a band of gold around a finger while neighbors had nothing to eat. His advice was "make all you can" and "save all you can" and "give all you can."

The Bible has always been clear that we are not our own cre-ations. We are made by a God of love. We are bid to die to all other allegiances other than the allegiance we make to Christ and to our brothers and sisters for whom Christ died.

Christians are asked to choose a special way of seeing and living in the world. This special way is one that constantly asks the question: What's in it for others? True, we live in a free country, and we can believe anything we want. But we can't worship the wrong things and have our lives turn out right! What's in it for others?

Our Christian organizations in this country are so responsive to human need that I imagine that many of you have significant stories about wake-up calls you received relative to human need. Marva Dawn had a wake up call that shook her to the core the summer after her junior year in college. She sang in a college choir traveling around the world. During the ten days the students spent in India, she was overwhelmed by the thousands of beggars and countless dead bodies in the streets. The students watched horri-fied as workers came and scooped the bodies into wheelbarrows to transport them to the dump to be burned. She says, "My naïve life was turned upside down." [8]

I think we are all aware of Jesus' principle that we should live our lives for others. But we wonder if people have historically done that, except for a few religious monks, ascetics, and saints. Can people really make major business and scientific decisions based on what's in it for others? One person boldly said to me, "No one acts on this principle, so what's the good of talking about it?"

Christian business men and women have acted on this principle of serving others before themselves for centuries. In fact, we are still benefiting from their generosity.

Much has been in the news recently about a mining tragedy. Heroic rescue workers gave their lives searching in vain for trapped co-workers. In 1816, Sir Humphry Davy, an English scientist, perfected the safety-lamp, which revolutionized the technique of mining. This little lamp has saved the lives of tens of thousands of coal miners. Sir Humphry did not patent the invention. He wanted it to become immediately available for everyone at a cheap price. A friend subsequently criticized him because he failed to patent the lamp: "You would have made a fortune if you had patented that lamp." To the criticism, Sir Humphry replied, "I never considered patenting the lamp. My sole object . . . was to serve humanity . . . I am amply rewarded by that gratifying recollection."[9]

One hundred years ago, two unsung scientists, Pierre and Marie Curie, informed the French Academy of their research that had led them to believe in the existence of radium. The scientific world laughed at them. The two scientists continued to perfect the process of isolating radium. Finally, the world believed in the existence of this previously unknown element.

Soon the Curies were faced with an incredible decision. If ever a couple had the chance to cash in and clean up, they did. Of all the people in the world, they alone knew the secret formula of this much-welcomed uranium product, which makes x-rays and radiation treatment of cancer possible today. The commercial value of radium was at that time $150,000 per gram. In today's value, that would be $9,600,000 per gram. And they were the only two people in the world who knew how to get it.

The couple sat at a table one night. Pierre gave two options to Marie: they could make the results of their research public; or they could copyright their findings, patent the process, and personally control the manufacture of radium throughout the world. After considerable discussion and meditation, they came to a magnanimous decision: "It belongs to mankind."[10]

Maire Curie was the only female to receive the Nobel Prize for Physics and Chemistry. She died from complications of working with radium. She did not ask, "What's in it for me?" She asked herself, "What's in it for others?"

Sometimes we get so anxious over our present worries and future concerns that we forget why we go to church. We don't go to church just for ourselves. Church is the Christian community, and it exists in order to worship God and to live out the commandment given by Jesus Christ to love God and to love your neighbor as yourself. Worshiping God means loving our neighbors. Christ came to meet people's needs. And Christ's church should be dedicated to the needs of people—their spiritual, physical, political, material, and economic needs.

We have to start where we live and branch out. We all live among people who have incredible needs for food and medicine. Christians are known for being a generous people. We need to keep before us the power that we have to do something about the hunger in the areas where we live and in the larger world. We can stop hunger. Hunger can also be stopped in our world if we can get through the problems of delivery, motivation, human greed, and world-wide political despotism. Stopping hunger isn't that financially expensive. The United Nations Development Program estimates that basic health and nutrition needs of the world's poorest people could be met for $13 billion more a year. The people of the United States and Europe spend more than that on pet food each year.

In the last 50 years, almost 400 million people worldwide have died from hunger or poor sanitation. This is *three* times the number of people who have been killed in all the wars fought on earth in the last 100 years.

We do not at present seem to be able to stop AIDS or cancer or war. But by God, we can feed the hungry, here and around the world. God may not hold us accountable for what we are unable to cure. But I can't imagine God not asking us why we did not do what was in our power to do to cure hunger.

We Christians believe that Jesus is the answer to many of the world's problems. Certainly Jesus is the answer. But what is the question we should be asking? "What's in it for me?" Or "What's in it for others?"

Who's Going To Get What?

—— *t h e   l e s s o n s* ——

Hagar bore Abram a son; and Abram named his son, whom Hagar bore, Ishmael.

And Abram said to God, "O that Ishmael might live in your sight!" God said, "No, but your wife Sarah shall bear you a son, and you shall name him Isaac. I will establish my covenant with him as an everlasting covenant for his offspring after him. As for Ishmael, I have heard you; I will bless him and make him fruitful and exceedingly numerous; he shall be the father of twelve princes, and I will make him a great nation. But my covenant I will establish with Isaac, whom Sarah shall bear to you at this season next year."

—Genesis 16:15; 17:18-21

"Here is my servant, whom I have chosen, my beloved, with whom my soul is well pleased. I will put my Spirit upon him, and he will proclaim justice to the Gentiles. He will not wrangle or cry aloud, nor will anyone hear his voice in the streets. He will not break a bruised reed or quench a smoldering wick until he brings justice to victory. And in his name the Gentiles will hope."

He knew what they were thinking and said to them, "Every kingdom divided against itself is laid waste, and no city or house divided against itself will stand."

—Matthew 12:15-21, 25

The worst fight I ever participated in occurred on a football field. It did not occur between hostile fans. In fact, it did not take place between two *opposing* teams. It took place between members of the same team, our Furman team. We were having a scrimmage, our defense against our offense. The quarterback was completing pass after pass. Our defensive backs, me included, were of the rather strong opinion that our linemen were not putting much of a pass rush on the quarterback. Little comments like, "The quarterback can write a letter to his mother or drink a cup of coffee while he is waiting to see if his receivers get open" were verbalized between the defensive backs.

On the other hand, our linemen were of the strong opinion that they couldn't rush because we were leaving the receivers open. Finally, a huge defensive tackle turned around to me and screamed, "Warlick, are ya'll going to start covering those guys?" I *might*, I don't remember exactly, have said something unpleasant to him about his size and lack of speed. Well, the next thing I knew, our strong safety had slugged the defensive tackle upside the helmet. Quick as a flash, our other defensive tackle leveled the strong safety in retaliation. For five or ten minutes, it was the worst argument and fight I ever saw. The coaches couldn't stop it.

When order was finally restored, penalty flags littered the field. But the referees were at a loss as to what to call. The best they could come up with was an unsportsmanlike conduct penalty and a delay of game penalty. Needless to say, as those grudges were nursed through the rest of the season, ours was very much a house divided for some of the remaining games.

The worst fights that ever take place are those between members of the same family. In our history, more American lives were lost in the Civil War than in all the other wars we have fought *combined*. There were over 30,000 families that lost a son fighting for each side. And look at our world today. The great tensions are not just between invading and defensive nations and superpowers, but between warring members of the same national family like North and South Korea, Iraq, Afghanistan, and much of Africa and Eastern Europe. Family fights are the worst kind. The worst fights are between family members over who is going to get what. If you cannot understand that, you cannot understand the Bible and the true miracle that was Jesus Christ. What's more, *you can never have peace of mind, true emotional and mental stability, until you understand the human race as part of your family and stop worrying about who's going to get what in life.* Perhaps in this regard, our Bible can be of genuine help to us.

The place to look is in the life of a man of faith who was not always a person of perfect character. The Bible is realistic about our father, Abraham. He was a human being, not a perfect saint. Occasionally he, like perhaps all of us, had some serious letdowns in his usual uprightness. The Bible tells us that there was a famine in the land so Abraham went down to Egypt to live where he could obtain food. As he journeyed, he began to worry. His wife, Sarah, was very beautiful. He feared that the Pharaoh might kill him and take his wife. So he decided to lie to Pharaoh and tell him that she was his sister. Abraham then sold Sarah to the Pharaoh. Fortunately,

Pharaoh learned the truth, gave Abraham a good lecture on ethics, and let her go. To say that Arab and Jew are inter-related is an under statement. If not for God's power and Pharaoh's ethics, there would be no children of Israel.

Well, Abraham's family problems had just started. Abraham and Sarah grew older, and they became painfully aware of their inability to have children. Sarah apparently despaired over her plight. She knew God had blessed Abraham and had promised him that he would be the father of a great nation. A scheme was the answer. She suggested to Abraham that he have a child by Hagar, their Egyptian servant. That was quite proper for the Bronze Age culture. Sarah reasoned with Abraham that "since Hagar is part of our household, it's the closest we can get to having our own child."

When Hagar became pregnant, Sarah told Abraham that the purpose had been accomplished and he was to go no more to Hagar. But Sarah began to resent Hagar and abused her. Hagar fled to the wilderness; and there God promised her a healthy baby, to be named Ishmael, and told her to go home in spite of Sarah. As the oldest son of father Abraham, Ishmael was the child of entitlement, the rightful heir of Abraham and God's promises. In fact, Scripture says that God had a special commitment to Ishmael.

As so often happens when people who can't have children make arrangements to secure a child, Sarah herself became pregnant. She gave birth to a boy, whom she named Isaac. Of course, Sarah abruptly ordered Hagar never to hold or touch her son, Isaac. All of Sarah's pent-up resentment came to a boil one day.

She ran into the house and pointed her finger in Abraham's face and screamed, "You drive out that slave and her son. I'm worried about who's going to get what. Listen. No son of that slave is going to share the inheritance with my son Isaac."

Obviously, Abraham was greatly distressed. He went out in the backyard and prayed. God told Abraham that God was well inclined toward both boys. God told Abraham that the descendants of Isaac would bear his name. But He also promised Abraham that He would make a great nation of Ishmael, since Ishmael was also Abraham's offspring. So the next morning, in great sorrow, Abraham gave the young Egyptian woman, Hagar, and their mutual son, Ishmael, some water and bread and sent them out into the wilderness.

After a few days, Hagar and Ishmael ran out of food and water. Hagar thought they would die. But God heard the little boy's cry and sent a messenger who pointed out a well of water.

Finally, Abraham died. Ishmael returned for his funeral and together with Isaac, his half-brother, they buried old Abraham in a cave. Now Abraham left a will. Even in death, he apparently continued his imperfection. You see, although he had seven children, Abraham left everything to his son, Isaac. That is the Judeo-Christian side of the story.

Abraham's choice between Isaac and Ishmael resulted in a relentless feud of warring cousins that has lasted 7000 years to this very day. The Jews trace their origins to Abraham through Isaac and Sarah. The Arabs go back to Abraham through Ishmael and Hagar and have God favoring that side of the family. The descendants of Abraham have never recognized each other as brothers and sisters. They are still fighting in the Middle East over who's going to get what.

Christians believe that after thousands of years spent watching his fallen, warring children, God sent his only son down among them to try to make them see that the human race is all one family under a living God. This Jesus was born a Jew and raised an Egyptian. Paul said it correctly, "God was in Christ reconciling the world back to him." And do you know what the world did with this Jesus? They started arguing again over who's going to get what.

Jesus gave a commandment—"love God and neighbor." Some questioned, "Who's my neighbor? Who's going to get this love?"

Jesus preached the resurrection. But the Sadducees came up to him and said, "Master, Moses said if a man dies, having no children, his brother shall marry his wife, have children, and raise up children. But suppose the man has seven brothers, and they each marry the woman, die in turn, and leave no children. In the resurrection whose wife will she be?" Who's going to get what? Jesus answered, "You do not understand; in the resurrection they neither marry nor are given in marriage, but are as the angels of God in heaven." In other words, you don't have to worry about who's going to get what because everybody gets it all.

Jesus told James and John to follow him, and they started talking with their parents. Finally, their mother came up to Jesus and asked if maybe her boys couldn't sit at the right and left hand of Jesus in heaven, in favored places, since there were 12 disciples and that's quite a crowd. In other words, who's going to get what?

Finally, a Samaritan woman was impressed with Jesus by a well one day. So she said, "Sire, there are three temples, one in Samaria, one in Jerusalem, and one in Egypt. Which one is the true one? Who's going to get what?" Jesus replied, "None of them. The true worshippers worship one Father in Spirit and in truth. God is a spirit. We are all one family."

Now, what do we make of all these family feuds? What is the Bible trying to tell us? In the first place, it means that God chooses us not because we are truthful, honest, and dependable. Do we merit God's choosing us and sending his son? The answer given from Genesis to Revelation is a resounding NO! We Christians, Baptists, Methodists, Americans, or whatever, are not righteous but sinners. We are not just created but fallen. The Son of God comes not to call the righteous but the fallen, fighting sinners. It's a gift.

Secondly, our history has proven that the Scriptures are right about what it takes to get peace of mind. Look at the Bible and all the misery caused by those who fought over who's going to get what. See how that fallen state affects our human condition even today.

The sociology department of Duke University years ago did a study on peace of mind. They isolated the factors that create emotional and mental stability. They were *(my response in italics)*:

1. The absence of suspicion and resentment. *(Nursing a grudge is a major factor in unhappiness.)*
2. Not living in the past. *(Who got what doesn't matter if you trust God. Do not be unwholesomely preoccupied with old mistakes and failures. Everybody gets everything in the long run.)*
3. Refuse to indulge in self-pity when life hands you a raw deal. Accept the fact that nobody gets through life without some sorrow and misfortune. *(Abraham didn't. Sarah didn't. Isaac and Ishmael didn't. Joseph and Mary didn't. Jesus didn't. And you won't either.)*
4. Find something bigger than yourself to believe in. *(Self-centered people, who are always worrying about who's going to get what, score lowest on tests for measuring happiness.)*

Can you imagine how powerful our lives would be if we stopped worrying about who's going to get what? Can you imagine what a world would be like where everybody stopped worrying about who's going to get what? Jesus said there is such a power, and there is such a place. It is called the Kingdom of God. And there is no greater peace than accepting his invitation to walk out of our present condition into that kingdom. It heals. It restores. It brings peace of mind.

PART FIVE

— *Peace Of Mind* —

Peace Of Mind

—— *the lesson* ——

Then Peter came and said to him, "Lord, if another member of the church sins against me, how often should I forgive? As many as seven times?" Jesus said to him, "Not seven times, but, I tell you, seventy-seven times."

—Matthew 18:21-22

T he teachings of Jesus are not always supposed to make us comfortable. They are meant to change our minds, change the way we live our lives and ultimately change our hearts. Neither are they meant to make us afraid. Jesus and his teachings are meant to re-center us. In this way, we can discover who we really are and to whom we ultimately belong, finding a much needed peace of mind.

Those who study nature tell us that we humans possess some of the same reactions to life as the animals. Consider the cottontail rabbit. It is a victim of *indiscriminate anxiety*. It cannot tell the difference between a friend and an enemy. Out in the woods, it runs as fast from a hiker carrying a walking stick as it does from a hunter holding a gun. With its morbid imagination, the bunny views every stranger as an enemy. It can't distinguish between good and evil.

The common crow of North America is quite different. It *can* discriminate. It will boldly fly up to an innocent, unarmed nature lover out for a walk. It knows that this person will do it no harm. The crow can tell the difference between a friend and a foe.[1]

If I could give all of us something, high on the list would be this: the ability to discriminate between those people and things in life that will harm us and those people and things in life that will help us. Indiscriminate anxiety is a horrible thing. To be in constant worry over real and imagined events is a sickness.

Jesus Christ actually made few claims. But one He did make was to give His followers peace of mind—not absence from failures, problems, and troubles—but peace of mind in the midst of those things. That seems strange when you consider that he was crucified, and so were most of his disciples.

One of the things a minister learns early in the practice of the profession is that there are three sides to every misunderstanding: yours, mine, and the truth. Eventually, you come to realize that this doesn't necessarily mean that anybody is lying. You never do find out who didn't do this or that or who misinterpreted whom. Events happen to people who each have their authoritative chronicles. Robert Capron is right: "Nobody is lying; it is just that their common history has fallen apart."[2]

I am convinced that the only way to experience peace of mind is to quit looking for just the human facts about ourselves and try to recover our history as children of God. In essence, that's what Jesus came to earth to do, to help us humans recover our history. "I am the truth and the life," He said. Then He told humans that our history is as follows: *God created us and created us to be good, in God's image: God is forgiving and we should be forgiving; God's yoke is easy, not hard, light and not heavy.*

We all know the human truth as we sit here in the 21st century. The world is torn to pieces. The Middle East is always aflame with violence. The Stock Market goes up and down and then way down. People make money, and people lose money. Our natural environment is in trouble. Oil is becoming a more limited resource than ever before, and climate change has the world in a frenzy. We have possession of the facts. But our anxiety occurs not when we are unaware of the facts. Our anxiety occurs when our history falls apart.

What exactly is our common history? The constant element running throughout the Bible is that our God is a forgiving

God. And if we were made in God's image, then we humans are never at rest until we, too, are forgiving people. Our human history is one of forgiveness. We were created by a forgiving God to be forgivers ourselves.

Once, Peter asked Jesus, "How often shall my brother sin against me, and I forgive him? As many as seven times?" Jesus answered, "I do not say to you seven times, but seventy-seven times." (Matthew 18:21-22). It seems to be an absurd answer. Few of us can even remember a friend who has wounded us three times, much less can we think of one who has "sinned" against us 77 times! Jesus was saying to Peter, "Your history is that of a forgiver." Your mind will never be at peace if you are always searching for the truth about the people who you think wronged you.

Even in the midst of his suffering, Jesus pointed humans toward an awareness that *God created us humans and created us to be good.* When Jesus enabled His followers to understand that, they never again lacked peace of mind regardless of their personal fortunes.

Craig Lambert, Deputy Editor of *Harvard Magazine*, wrote an incisive article about psychology entitled, "The Science of Happiness."[3] He noted that much of the history of psychology had seemed to be obsessed with pathology and failings of human beings. In fact, the very idea of psychology as formulated by Freud was profoundly pessimistic about human nature. Lambert concluded that positive psychology is needed to go beyond defining conditions that induce depraved behavior and actually seek to define conditions that foster generosity, creativity, and peace of mind.

Decades ago, H.T. Webster, a newspaper cartoonist, amused himself one day by sending telegrams to 20 acquaintances he selected at random. Each telegram simply read "Congratulations!" As far as Webster knew, not one of them had received any honor on which to be congratulated. Yet each took the message and wrote him a letter of thanks. Each person had done something that he or she regarded as worthy of some special praise.

If God created us to be good, then there is always a place for us, always a contribution we each can make to life. A "heritage, a niche in life," it is called. And finding this niche, this heritage, brings peace of mind. The tragedy is that sometimes we forget how important that niche can be.

Marcus Bach conveyed a compelling story about a restaurant in the state of Montana where, for 18 years, people made it a point to stop for a piece of homemade pie. Everybody seemed to stop with the pie in mind. The restaurant was always full. Even when calorie counting became a trend, customers still left room for a big slice of homemade pie of whatever kind was waiting fresh on the immaculate shelves.

The genius behind it all was a plump, motherly woman who always wore a clean white apron. Her name was Mamie. Through the years, Mamie's restaurant grew. Soon a service station was built nearby. Then a grocery store and a motel were constructed. Eventually, a gift shop and a zoo for the passing motorists sprang up.

Mamie apparently didn't quite realize all that was happening. Finally, her smile began to have a touch of sadness. Then one day, a wealthy tourist complimented Mamie on her pies. Mamie responded, "But that's all l can do—just bake pies."

Several summers later, something happened. Mamie left. The pies were still pies but not the kind and quality that Mamie used to bake. Mamie's absence gave the customers that let down feeling. Year after year, fewer cars stopped, for Mamie had gone.

Her only reason for leaving was her comment, "That's all I can do—just bake pies." So she sold the restaurant. The settlement rapidly deteriorated. The gift shop closed; the zoo folded; there was a "For Lease" notice on the grocery store. The final demise in the death of the settlement was signaled by a plywood plaque on the restaurant door, "For Sale - Inquire Within."[4]

The crossroads, where so many used to time their trips to rest awhile, stood empty. Bach noted that the walls and doors seemed to point toward the lonely sky and wail, "Come back, Mamie, come back! Please come home, Mamie."[5] Mamie had moved to a more progressive city. That's the truth. But *she lost her history.*

To a world chased out of Eden with no sense of importance, a Savior came. To a world interested in an eye-for-an-eye and a tooth-for-a-tooth, a Savior came. To a world desperate over indiscriminate anxiety—fearful of its sins and failures, guilty of its transgressions, running like a scared rabbit down the dark halls of life, a Savior came. As he marched toward the pain of his cross to be crucified, Jesus uttered the plaintive cry, "Come back, O world, please come back. Come back to your history. Your God who made you made you good and who judges you, is a forgiving, loving God. Your history, your heritage, is one of loving, forgiving and trusting. I tell you your history. And in that telling, I give you a peace. Not as the world gives peace give I unto you—but a peace that passes all understanding."

How do we achieve peace of mind? We recover our history. We remember the Savior who died for us. We recover our history of goodness and forgiveness, and we remember that God's yoke is easy, not hard. When we let Jesus tell us who we are and what we are to be about, we find true peace of mind. We become re-centered so that we do not walk away from the best thing that ever happened to us, our history of being good and our knowledge of a crucified and risen savior, Jesus Christ, our Lord. That is really good news.

Good News For Good Living

— *the lessons* —

In the morning David wrote a letter to Joab, and sent it by the hand of Uriah. In the letter he wrote, "Set Uriah in the forefront of the hardest fighting, and then draw back from him, so that he may be struck down and die." As Joab was besieging the city, he assigned Uriah to the place where he knew there were valiant warriors. The men of the city came out and fought with Joab; and some of the servants of David among the people fell. Uriah the Hittite was killed as well.

—*II Samuel 11:14-17*

For I handed on to you as of first importance what I in turn had received: that Christ died for sins in accordance with the scriptures, and that he was buried, and that he was raised on the third day in accordance with the scriptures, and that he appeared to Cephas, then to the twelve. Then he appeared to more than five hundred brothers and sisters at one time, most of whom are still alive, though some have died. Then he appeared to James, then to all the apostles. Last of all, as to one untimely born, he appeared also to me. For I am the least of the apostles, unfit to be called an apostle, because I persecuted the church of God. But by the grace of God I am what I am, and his grace toward me has not been in vain.

—*I Corinthians 15:3-10*

y wife and I both grew up in Augusta, Georgia, so we have been to the Masters golf tournament many times. The last time she and I went together to the Masters was about 15 years ago. We went immediately to what we call "our spot," below the elevated sixth tee, a par three where the golfers hit over the heads of spectators down to the green. Two young college students came and sat next to us. The young man was blond and well-built. He was holding hands with a pretty girl. I noticed a huge, ornate ring on the right hand of the young fellow. I inquired about the ring. He informed me that it was given to him for playing on the conference championship football team at Furman University, where he was a student. The student introduced the girl beside him as his fiancée and a member of the Furman dance team.

Diane leaned over and whispered to me, "This is eerie. They are the same age as we were when we first met, and they attend the same college from which we graduated. It's like we are sitting beside ourselves as we used to be."

I spoke to the young man: "I used to play football at that school, too." The young man responded, "Yes sir." Diane interjected, "And I used to be a member of the dance team there, too." The coed looked at her and said, "Yes ma'am." After a barrage of "yes sirs, no sirs, yes ma'ams, and no ma'ams," we felt old, as if we were sitting beside our replacements in life.

I forgot the golf tournament and thought about the resurrection of Jesus and its claims. No longer was it fodder for a sermon I could preach to skeptical doubters who had lost loved ones. No longer was it a ready resource for counseling techniques that could bring assurances to complex biomedical decisions about when is the time to let go of a loved one. The claims for the resurrection of Jesus Christ had a newfound urgency. The question was no longer "What's going to happen to *you* when *you* die or what happened to my parents when *they* died?"

All it took was a few "yes sirs" and "no sirs" to snap the issue around to "What's going to happen to *me* when *I* die?" And it hasn't gotten better in the intervening years. Whoever said that life is like a roll of toilet paper, is correct. The closer you get to the end, the faster it seems to get used up.

Each summer Sunday, the worshippers at the seasonal church where I minister start their formal worship service by saying together the Apostle's Creed—which states that Jesus will come again, "to judge the quick and the dead." The earliest meaning of the word "quick" in English is "alive." When a baby was first felt to move in its mother's womb, usually about the 26th week, it was considered to have come to life, and this moment was called "the quickening." Ultrasound technology made it possible to see that a fetus is in motion even if the pregnant woman does not yet feel it. The phrase "the quick and the dead" is kept alive by the King James translation of Acts 10:42 and our traditional recitations of the Apostles' Creed. To me, the good news for my living and dying is this: the one God has chosen to judge us humans, whether at 26 weeks or 100 years after death, is Jesus.

Today's text from Corinthians is the oldest text in the New Testament. Paul quotes a confessional creed used by the early church.

Christ died for our sins in accordance with the Scriptures.

- He was buried.

- He was raised on the third day in accordance with the Scriptures.

- He appeared to Cephas, to the 12, to more than 500 people at one time, to James and all the apostles, and last of all, to Paul.

This Pauline repetition of the good news is also our bridge for unlocking the secrets of the human condition. Paul touches all the bases. Like us, he implies that he has had no earthly contact with Jesus. Paul calls the list of those who witnessed the resurrection and asserts that "some have died." He notifies his charges that "last of all he appeared to me." Apparently, resurrection appearances are over. He is transmitting a tradition that is a summary of the proclamation of the early church.

The burial confirms a death. The appearances confirm the means by which the resurrection is perceived. The creed affirms two profound aspects of Jesus—his total humanity and his intense closeness to God. This is not only our Rosetta Stone for unlocking the mysteries of human life, it is a new entryway to God, a new access point, a new exit ramp at the end of the freeway of life, so to speak. Our replacements are already upon the earth. As Camus says, "The human being is the only animal that knows it's going to die."

We who are to die and be buried or cremated are, through Jesus, intensely close to God and have been since our first movements. As Paul labors to preach it, Jesus was not just killing time with his ministry of teaching and healing until he could get to the resurrection as the main event. The resurrection is filled with meaning precisely because it is illuminated by everything Jesus had taught with his words and actions as a human being who died and was buried.

Paul restates that tradition to the divided Corinthians—"This is what we preach and this is what you believed" (v. 11). This is the ultimate hope of the world. We can have hope for the whole human race because with God, things are straightened out and made known for both the quick and the dead. Since life certainly is often not fair, we cannot underestimate the importance of the death of Jesus on the cross. We see a good man crucified on a slab of wood as a monument to the price that conscience pays when it does not square with what the world requires.

There is another Scripture listed with this chapter. It is an upsetting story to read. King David wants to cover up his affair with Bathsheba and also steal her from her husband, Uriah the Hittite, one of David's most loyal soldiers. David writes a letter to Joab, the head of his troops. David has got to get rid of this good and popular man, Uriah. So he tells Joab to put Uriah in the forefront of the hardest fighting and then have everyone draw back from him so he will be killed. And it happens. Joab follows orders. Uriah is killed. Life isn't always fair in love or war.

One of the most enjoyable and intimidating places where I have preached in North America is Harvard's Memorial Church. The Memorial Church is the church for Harvard University. It was dedicated on Armistice Day 1932 in memory of those who died in World War I, a gift of the alumni to the University. Memorials have been added to remember those who have died in the wars since. Consequently, the entire right wall of the sanctuary has chiseled in granite the names of all the 697 Harvard men and Radcliffe women who died in America's declared wars from World War I through the Vietnam War. That's intimidating. At least the Vietnam War Memorial in Washington, with all its names, is outdoors where you can get away. But when the names of the dead from the undergraduate class of 1880 to the class of 1970 are surrounding you, your preaching had better say something.

Amid that sea of 697 names, listed by the war in which they were killed and their class year and school, is one name that has an asterisk by it. Two divinity school graduates were killed in World

War II and one of them, Adolf Sannwald, has an asterisk beside his name with the notation "Enemy Casualty." For three decades, I looked at that name and thought, how liberal and benevolent that such a generous university would remember a fallen son who had fought for the opposition. On more than one occasion, graduates of some of the other schools would deride the name of the lone German and make a condescending remark about the Divinity School, such as, "Half the men who died fighting in World War II from the Divinity School were on the wrong side. I guess they always have been a contentious bunch."[6]

The newspaper of Los Altos, California, the hometown of the Silicon Valley, carried an article entitled "Adolf Sannwald: The Story Behind An Enemy Casualty." It noted that Sannwald studied at the Divinity School during the 1920's. In 1930, he accepted a prestigious call as pastor of St. Mark's Lutheran Church in Stuttgart. As early as 1931, he angered the National Socialists with his sermons. When Hitler sought control of the Protestant churches through his German Christian Movement, which forced Protestant churches to merge and support Nazi ideology, Sannwald joined the confessing church, an underground Christian resistance movement that opposed the German leader.

In 1934, he wrote in a pamphlet, "God did not choose his children on the basis of race. We may not and will not confuse faith in Jesus Christ with some other faith in a religious or political world view."[7]

Warned that the Gestapo had ordered his arrest, Sannwald accepted a call to a tiny church in the Black Mountains where he felt his family would be safe. He protected local Jews by sheltering them in the church rectory. By 1942, the government had located him. In January, he was arrested. Rather than sending him to prison, which would have created problems due to Sannwald's popularity with the people, they did what David did to Uriah. They drafted him as a common soldier, and three days later put him on a train to the

Russian front. He was never allowed to serve as a chaplain because he refused to join the Nazi Party and was permitted to preach only once to his fellow soldiers on the way. When he got to Russia, they immediately gave him a gun, which he probably never learned how to fire, and put him in the forward trench where wounded and badly frostbitten, he was killed in an air raid.

I knew some of the story because on the 50th anniversary of the end of World War II, the minister of Memorial Church, Reverend Peter Gomes, had heard parts of the truth from Sannwald's relatives. He immediately went to the secretary of the university to try to get something done about it. The Harvard authorities said, "Well, he died in combat as a member of the German army." In bureaucratic frustration, the secretary asked, "How many asterisks can we put up?" So the name stands—a monument to the price a human pays when his or her conscience goes against the society. Aren't we glad that it is Jesus and not the world or its leaders who will judge the quick and the dead?[8]

The good news for good living is this: Jesus will be the judge of humankind. And we know how Jesus judges people—with kindness and mercy beyond anything we know or have experienced. I have scoured the Bible and its lists—from the begets of the Old Testament, to the family tree of Jesus in Matthew, to the statement in the book of Revelation of the 144,000 unfit that are allowed into the Kingdom of Heaven after the saints have gone in, to all the witnesses listed as saints and forbearers of ours in the Epistle to the Hebrews, to Paul's lists of his followers, to the 12 and the 72 sent out by Jesus and to the 500 witnesses of the resurrection. I have found scoundrels, saints, foreigners, prostitutes, unsavory characters, and common folks galore. But *I haven't found an asterisk beside a single name.* Not one. There won't be one by your name, either. Let's leave here with joy and live the rest of our lives working to implement the teachings and practices of Jesus. *He* will judge the quick and the dead.

Put Out into the Deep Water

— *the lessons* —

When he had finished speaking, he said to Simon, "Put out into the deep water and let down your nets for a catch." Simon answered, "Master, we have worked all night long but have caught nothing. Yet if you say so, I will let down the nets." When they had done this, they caught so many fish that their nets were beginning to break. So they signaled their partners in the other boat to come and help them. And they came and filled both boats, so that they began to sink.

–Luke 5:4-7

But when God, who had set me apart before I was born and called me through his grace, was pleased to reveal his Son to me, so that I might proclaim him among the Gentiles, I did not confer with any human being, nor did I go up to Jerusalem to those who were already apostles before me, but I went away at once into Arabia, and afterwards I returned to Damascus.

Then after three years I did go up to Jerusalem to visit Cephas and stayed with him fifteen days; but I did not see any other apostle except James the Lord's brother. In what I am writing to you, before God, I do not lie!

–Galatians 1:15-20

S ometimes the best advice can come from the most unlikely places. When I first began my ministry, I was pastor of a church in a small town. The first week, an elderly woman, a retired insurance agent who taught the middle-aged ladies Sunday School class, called me at the church. She said, "Sometime when it is convenient for you, please come by my house. I have some advice I want to give to you. I neglected to give it to your predecessor, and he bombed out."

Obviously, I replied, "Where do you live? I will be by there in five minutes." We both sat in rocking chairs on her front porch, and she gave me the following advice. "Don't read what we read," she implored. "We read Reader's Digest; we read the local newspaper; we read the best selling novels; we read *Time Magazine*; we read the *Wall Street Journal*; we attend Bible studies, and we read the material associated with them. We are counting on you to read better stuff than that." Then she continued, "Please read deeper material than we do. On Sunday morning, you can then take us somewhere that we could not have gotten to on our own." She concluded, " We all need to reason and work together at a genuine and deep level so we can get things done and not just be engaged in catching minnows in shallow water."

That's quite a gauntlet to have thrown down before you. Superficial attention-grabbing statements would not cut it with her.

Even in churches, I have seen some amazing and shallow gimmicks used to try to grab people's attention and get them to attend. Two weeks before Easter one year, an Assembly of God church in Indiana released "One Thousand Resurrection Helium Balloons." Inside these balloons were gift certificates to local stores ranging in value up to $75. The certificates had to be presented in person in Sunday School on Easter Sunday at the church to be redeemed.

When it comes to long-term and deep thinking, consider some of the obstacles that have to be overcome by today's children who have entered college since the year 2000. They are called Millennials. They live by text messages and e-mails and form much of their knowledge about life from three-second television sound bytes. They have participated in virtually every sport and activity known to humankind and been given trophies for just showing up. They know they are special, and they want special treatment. They can handle busy schedules, but uncertainty throws them. If their teacher doesn't tell them what is going to be on a test, they go into orbit. And as for reading something, why should you care about anything that isn't going to be on the exam?

It is so important for people in our world to engage with each other at a deeper level than staring down, plugging in and dropping out. Gazing into a Blackberry or looking at a Twitter certainly matches our setting and embodies our desires, but it doesn't take the place of staring into someone's eyes and having them with you. Certainly, technology is efficient, and I do not reject those gifts. But sometimes we have to be together and engage each other. Charles Kuralt and Bob Timberlake put together an album and book of paintings that began, "Let me tell you of a time when people lived farther apart but were closer together."

Sometimes we have to move beyond ideological segregation

and have meaningful discussions with people who disagree with us, so we can become closer together in our hope for the future and in our understanding of other people. The University of Pennsylvania recently conducted a survey of 12 countries and found that Americans are the least likely to talk about politics and major national issues with those who disagree with them. One of the greatest dangers facing any society is superficiality and closed mindedness.

Today's scripture recognizes that. Jesus is by a lake along the Sea of Galilee. He sees two boats. He gets into the one owned by Simon Peter. They stay near the shore, and Jesus teaches the people from the boat. When he finishes speaking, Jesus, says to the disciples, "Put out into the deep water and let your nets down for a catch."

Now, these were professional fishermen. Peter and James and John were owners of boats. The father of James and John, a man named Zebedee, owned a whole fleet of boats. These professionals had been fishing all night and had caught nothing. Jesus said, "Put out into the deep water and let down your nets there." Even with all their professionalism, they apparently had been fishing too shallow. When they went deep and let down the nets, they filled two boats, and those boats began to sink they were so full. Everyone was astonished at the size of the catch of fish. When the boats began to sink, all of them were afraid. And Jesus said, "Don't be afraid; from now on you will be catching people." Verse 11 of that fifth chapter of Luke ends with the disciples bringing their boats to shore and leaving everything they owned to follow Jesus. They had found someone with some depth.

Do you know what happened next? The very next verse, verse 12, was one where Jesus showed them how to go deep and fish for people. Read it sometime. They came upon a man in a circle of people, and the man had leprosy. He cried out to Jesus, "I believe you can heal me if you want to." Jesus responded, "I want to heal you; be healed." Jesus touched a leper, a person who the Jewish religion considered to be unclean. Jesus got his hands dirty. Jesus talked with and touched someone his religion was afraid of. You could die working among lepers. Jesus was taking the disciples into deep water. And that is where they would find the people they were fishing for. The word spread all over the known world: "This teacher touches everybody. This man isn't just for the Jews alone. This person can go deeper than his own religious tradition and overcome the worst situations in the world." Small wonder, then, that people started flocking to see and hear him in person.

To me, one of the saddest decisions ever made by mainline Protestantism was its false assertion that in order to reach this generation, we should give them attractive but superficial expressions of faith, music, and the Word of God. When faced with a largely unchurched public, somebody decided we needed to dumb down our worship services and preaching and start fishing in shallow waters. And it hasn't worked for our churches anymore than it has worked in the field of politics, which dumbed down its presentations of candidates to a series of televised sound bytes decades ago.

One of the significant issues in Luke's account of Jesus trying to pull the disciples into deeper thoughts, purposes, and healings concerns his instructions to the leper he healed. The Scriptures are clear: "And Jesus ordered him to tell no one. 'Go,' he said, 'and show yourself to the priest and . . . make an offering for your cleansing, for a testimony to them.'"

In other words, don't gloat about it—your real testimony is helping support those causes and people who made it possible for God's work to be done for you. Just do it. If you have been healed, live like it. That's your testimony. Go deep with your own life and your own contributions to the faith that has healed you.

After this event, the Bible tells us that Jesus became more popular than ever. So often, we talk about what Jesus did for others. But it is evident that the faith of others had an important impact on him as well. Here at the beginning of his ministry, the faith of a leper turns his career around. And Jesus' willingness to stop and listen to a person that others considered unclean and unreligious showed his disciples just how deep his love was.

Listening to, talking with, and embracing the hopes of others who are as different from you as night is from day are critical to healing, for both the giver and the receiver. Greg Mortenson has written a best-selling book called *Three Cups of Tea*.[9] Tom Brokaw calls it "one of the most remarkable stories of our time." It is the dangerous and difficult story of Mortenson's quest to build schools for children in the wildest parts of the mountains of Afghanistan and Pakistan. It's basically how one person with the right character can literally change a world. Mortenson spends a lot of time listening to Muslims in that part of the world. The most influential is a man named Haji Ali.

This Muslim leader came up to him and told him before they started any project, that Mortenson had to make time to share three cups of tea with him. He told him that the cups, which had to be drunk in separate visits, symbolized being a stranger, being an honored guest, and, finally, being a part of the family. Haji Ali said we must make time to talk and visit. He explained, "Doctor Greg, we may be uneducated. But we are not stupid. We have lived here a long time."

Mortenson contends that was the most important lesson he learned in his life—to slow down, to listen to people, and to realize that building relationships is as important as building projects. He credits Haji Ali with teaching him that he had more to learn from the people he worked with than he could ever hope to teach them.

A great theologian named Paul Tillich once said that the first duty of loving somebody is to listen to them. If you love someone, you listen to them even if you don't want to hear what they say. That is what relationships are about. I will listen to you, if I love you. Jesus listened to the leper before he healed him; Jesus listened to the Samaritan woman by the well before he affirmed her; Jesus listened to the thief on the cross before he promised him a place in paradise; Jesus listened to the centurion before he healed his daughter; Jesus listened and loved first—then he worked on his projects.

Two of the most pivotal figures in the Bible are Jeremiah in the Old Testament and the apostle Paul in the New Testament. Jeremiah was the first to ask the question, "Why do the wicked sometimes prosper and the good sometimes experience bad things?" He was the first to fish in deeper water than the simple but effective traditional religious belief that rich and healthy people were that way because they were better than poor and unhealthy people. He, in short, made it possible for the way to be paved for a Messiah who suffered and was poor, to be accepted as a son of God.

Paul, of course, was the one who saved the church from provincialism and destruction by opening the message of Christ to the rest of the world and arguing that Jesus was for more than just the Jewish people. Both Jeremiah and Paul had a trait in common. They listened well to the world they were trying to reach. Jeremiah conducted a two-year long "listening-in campaign" before he began some of his greatest statements. He did not utter a word in public during a two year period. He listened to the people he was going to speak to and learned from them before he attempted to speak the Word of God to them.

Paul went deeper out to sea to fish than even Jeremiah did. In his own hand, Paul wrote these words in the first chapter of Galatians: "When God called me through his grace and revealed his Son to me so that I might proclaim him to the Gentiles . . . I did not go up to Jerusalem to those who were already apostles before me, but I went away at once to Arabia, and afterwards I returned to Damascus. Then after three years, I did go up to Jerusalem to visit Peter and stayed with him fifteen days; but I did not see any other apostle except James, the Lord's brother. In what I am writing to you, I swear to God I do not lie!" (Galatians 1: 15-20).

Paul spent three years in Arabia and what is now Turkey

learning from the people other apostles viewed as godless practitioners of other religions, Paul listened to the people of Arabia before he went back with the news of Christ. He loved them first. That is taking the boat into the deep waters. The catch was phenomenal.

Can you imagine what problems could be solved if the Democrats thought that they had more to learn from the Republicans than they had to teach them, and the Republicans thought they had more to learn from the Democrats than they had to teach them? What if our congressional representatives at every level actually listened to the people they disagree with or do not understand and admitted it, instead of fishing in the shallow waters of lobbyists, perception managers, and personal attacks? No telling what they might catch in their nets if they were brave enough to put out into the deep water.

We need a big vision. We need some deep thinkers. We need people to get away from their comfortable shores and listen to the people they believe they should be teaching. May God help us in this global and crowded world to always dare to seek new depths of meaning.

The Goodness and
Wonder of You

—— *the lessons* ——

When I look at your heavens, the work of your fingers, the moon and the stars that you have established; what are human beings that you are mindful of them, mortals that you care for them?

Yet you have made them a little lower than God, and crowned them with glory and honor. You have given them dominion over the works of your hands; you have put all things under their feet, all sheep and oxen, and also the beasts of the field, the birds of the air, and the fish of the sea, whatever passes along the paths of the seas.

O Lord, our Sovereign, how majestic is your name in all the earth!

—Psalm 8:3-9

The word that came to Jeremiah from the Lord: Come, go down to the potter's house, and there I will let you hear my words." So I went down to the potter's house, and there he was working at his wheel. The vessel he was making of clay was spoiled in the potter's hand, and he reworked it into another vessel, as seemed good to him.

Then the word of the Lord came to me: Can I not do with you, O house of Israel, just as this potter has done? says the Lord. Just like the clay in the potter's hand, so are you in my hand, O house of Israel.

—Jeremiah 18:1-6

T he first student assistant I had at High Point University, where I have taught and preached for more than two decades, was a lovely young woman, 21 years old. She was a bright, friendly student and very much involved in her social sorority. She spent a great deal of her time with another female student, also 21 years old, whose parents lived in our city. One weekend, my assistant was supposed to go to a party with this friend. Her own schedule conflicted at the last minute so her friend went without her to the party at the hotel on Main Street.

Just after the party ended that night, her friend was strangled to death in the parking garage of that hotel. The murderer, who later was given the death penalty in our state and in two other states for past crimes, was a total stranger. He just happened to be passing through town when the girl walked into the garage.

The next day, I sat on my front porch with the student assistant, who was obviously quite shaken. With a blank stare she kept saying, "I feel so small, so meaningless. You have no control over your life. Sometimes it's just luck. I was supposed to have gone to that party. I would have been right there with her. I would have been murdered, too. We're all so pitifully helpless."

In less dramatic fashion, sometimes our culture can conspire to make us feel despondent and pitifully helpless. The universe seems so vast; government seems so big and impersonal; the huge malls eliminate the mom-and-pop stores; and the job market seems so foreboding. Even in religion, the mega-churches and televisions have crippled the face-to-face congregations. Call it pluralism or urbanity; sometimes we are aware of our smallness in a big world. So foreboding is this prospect that many call themselves "survivalists" and move to western and mountainous states to live as vigilantes. Others around the world become suicidal bombers to feel in control against their big, evil, and threatening world.

Consider some of the ways you and I have been taught to devalue ourselves--to move away from thinking that we are, indeed, special and wonderful and good.

With each new and larger telescope and with each successful flight into outer space, the universe seems to get bigger, and human life seems to get smaller and smaller. Instead of being special as the darlings of God, many believe that we humans are just the latest arrival in a long progression of lifeforms on a planet that is rolling around the sun with boring regularity. Some begin to see themselves as *mere* humans.

If that isn't belittling enough, sometimes psychology comes along and tries to reduce us to a bundle of conditioned reflexes. We are told that who we are depends on where we've been. As a baby we are "candidates for personality," with an "Oedipus complex" when a son has affection for his mother or a "father fixation" when a daughter pays attention to her father.[10] Some people are suspicious of every good deed people want to do for them and of the motivations behind all love and tenderness. In the midst of bad decisions then, we can always cop out with, "Hey, don't blame me. I'm *only* human."

Even being in college can sometimes make people feel small and vulnerable. In the face of all that stands on our college campus a chapel that asserts that we are all special; that we are good; that we need to believe in ourselves as created children of a good God and that God is mindful of us as individuals. We try to reaffirm what Psalm 8 preaches: the wonder and grandeur of human life.

Alfred North Whitehead said, "Moral education is impossible apart from the habitual vision of greatness." In other words, if we can't see ourselves as wonderful and good, it's virtually impossible to be moral, no matter how many courses we take in values or ethics or religion or philosophy or whatever. If we can't see *ourselves* as wonderful and good, how can we see *strangers* as wonderful and good? We tend to mirror people that we admire. That's essentially what worship is about—you and I looking up and seeing something great and good and wonderful *in whose image we are also created.*

The Old Testament, in several places, pictures God as a potter, creating each of us like a potter molding a beautiful object out of what amounts to mud. We are made out of clay, not chiseled out of rock. We are not hard and rigid, but malleable so God and life can mold us and use us. Jeremiah speaks of God being like a potter who shapes his vase and stands back and says, "This is good," and keeps on reshaping it, over and over so that it will be even better. Basically, this means that you and I are created with material that gives us the potential of changing for the better. God allows u-turns. That's what makes us unique and special. We get to learn the wonder and goodness of human life as we grow. That's our purpose on this earth.

William Beebe wrote about nature. He regretted the fact that no one had ever written an epic about the most dramatic thing in nature: *the law of compensation.* The law of compensation applies in both the animal and human realms. Each of us has certain limitations, but life also gives each of us an outstanding compensating ability. Beebe studied birds. He noticed that there is *one thing* each bird can do with superlative skill. The peacock has a wretched squawk that is the ugliest voice among birds. The peacock would

make an "F" in a singing contest. But on dress parade, it has no
rivals, for its display of color is incomparable. The nightingale
has the ugliest gray feathers among birds. It's an unattractive little
thing—until it sings. It possesses the most soul-stirring voice ever
heard. And the albatross walks so awkwardly along a sandy beach
that Beebe stated it moves "as though each step (brings it) acute
agony." But a few feet above the beach it is the master flyer, incomparable to all of nature. This is the law of compensation.[11] All of
God's creatures have an element of wonder and goodness. Admit-
tedly, sometimes that is very hard to see, but it is there if we look
hard enough.

Jesus the Christ taught people to see their wonder and goodness.
No one had ever done that before quite like He did. Jesus came to
Matthew and said, "Matthew, you're not just a tax collector. You are
wonderful, and you are good." He focused on Mary Magdalene and
said, "Mary, you're not just a common woman; you are wonderful,
and you are good." He spoke to Peter: "You're not just a tempera-
mental, volatile, redneck fisherman. You are wonderful, and you are
good." To the abuser Saul, he said, "You're not just an educated, conservative thug. You are wonderful, and you are good." To all of them
he said, "God has given you life. Do something godly with it."

The makings of a great life include deficiencies, troubles, and
even moral failures. But there is a force that can recreate us, empower
us, enable us to endure what we have to endure, and shape us to
become what we can become.

We have our university chapel services on Wednesday
evenings. At most colleges, including ours, Wednesday night has
become the biggest drinking night of the week. I fully realize, as
Dean of Chapel, that many of the student worshippers, including
some members of the chapel choir and some of those students who
lead the prayers, will be among the horde at some local bar. We try
to lift them up, seeing better people than they might see themselves
at that time in their lives. Most of the time, they at some point,

often after they graduate, juxtapose the chapel with the bar when they remember Wednesday nights. Most of them begin to get a glimpse of their goodness and wonder, and that creates something positive in their lives.

Not long ago, I performed a wedding in northern Maryland in which the bride was a recent graduate of High Point University. The wedding took place in an old, beautiful Lutheran church that was packed with more than 300 guests. In addition to the High Point graduates in the large wedding party, two long pews were filled with 17 young ladies from the bride's sorority. As I walked out of the church, one of the girls said, "This was neat. It felt like being back in chapel on a Wednesday night to all of us."

At the wedding reception, my wife and I sat down for the dinner with two family members of a young woman who had graduated from the university that spring. I had seen the couple in our chapel a few times over the years and had even eaten lunch with them after the graduation ceremonies that spring.

I had no idea what the man did for a living, but I assumed he was retired. He lamented that my wife and I had to leave the next morning to drive back to High Point because he had wanted to show us around. I asked what he did. He told me that he was the owner of a business that provided lumber and millwork for construction. In fact, he said, "We just got through remodeling Camp David, which is only two miles from here." I was fascinated, so I asked him to continue. "My grandfather started the lumber and millwork business in the late 1880's," he proudly stated. "Then it was passed to my father and then to me."

I urged him to tell me more. "We are the best at what we do," he intoned. "People trust us, and we have grown to where we have 70 acres under roof and 136 mill working stations. We send our people and our material all over the country when people need the best. Every President of the United States since 1900 has remodeled Camp David, and we have been the ones to do it. This past

President had us remodel it twice. We will start gearing up soon to remodel it again." With a twinkle in his eye he said, "We do lumber and millwork really well. That's our legacy."

Then, he leaned back and looked over at the back wall of the huge banquet room in which we were seated. All the girls who had attended our University, 22 of them, were stretched along that wall taking pictures and having fun. They came from Maryland, West Virginia, Massachusetts, and Kentucky. He leaned over to me and said, "Your students at High Point do Chapel really, really well. That's quite a legacy your university has. We go all over the country, and we don't see anything like it anywhere else."

The goodness and wonder of you is a very powerful thing.

The Silent Voice Of Peace

—— *t h e   l e s s o n s* ——

Now when they saw the boldness of Peter and John and realized they were uneducated and ordinary men, they were amazed and recognized them as companions of Jesus.

—Acts 4:13

One of the two who heard John speak and followed him was Andrew, Simon Peter's brother. He first found his brother Simon and said to him, "We have found the Messiah," (which is translated Anointed). He brought Simon to Jesus, who looked at him and said, "You are Simon son of John. You are to be called Cephas" (which is translated Peter).

The next day Jesus decided to go to Galilee. He found Philip and said to him, "Follow me." Now Philip was from Bethsaida, the city of Andrew and Peter. Philip found Nathanael and said to him, "We have found him about whom Moses in the law and also the prophets wrote, Jesus son of Joseph from Nazareth." Nathaniel said to him, "Can anything good come out of Nazareth?" Philip said to him, "Come and see."

—John 1:40-46

H ave you ever noticed the power of someone's presence among you? Some people don't have to say anything to be powerful. They just have to be there. Some of the most important and influential people in human history have been people whose words are not recorded to any great degree, if at all.

I realized this early in life when I was but 13 years old. That Christmas, I was asked to be in the Christmas pageant at the First Baptist Church of North Augusta, South Carolina. I was assigned to play the part of Joseph, the father of Jesus. That was a hard part to play. I kept trying to do something with the character. Every time I tried to do something, the director would say, "No, Harold, just stand there. Joseph isn't supposed to *do* anything; just stand there." Well, I figured if I couldn't act, I would at least say something. At the dress rehearsal when the curtains opened, being the father of Jesus, I said "Welcome to the manger at Bethlehem. Welcome to our house. Come see our baby." The director yelled, "Joseph isn't supposed to *do* anything. Joseph isn't supposed to *say* anything. Joseph just stands there. Do it."

I guess that's the way most of us see Joseph. Yet without Joseph, the story of Jesus' life would have unfolded differently. The silent, strong attitude of the man who named Jesus was itself a miracle among many miracles. Here was a man who awoke amidst his worse nightmare. He inherited a mess beyond description. But Joseph was a compassionate and just person. Before the angel came to him, he wanted to put Mary away privately. But the Law was very clear and very firm. It said that a man who had a suspiciously pregnant wife was supposed to put his wife to a public trial, expose her and stone her to death. Joseph went beyond the law. He wanted to treat Mary with compassion. He offered to divorce her and let her go quietly away.

Joseph, the father of Jesus, did not say anything at the birth of Jesus or even later that has been recorded. He was not a shouter. He was not an arguer. He was a strong and silent figure. He made sure that no person or any influence kept Jesus from fulfilling his destiny. He gave the child the freedom to grow up and become what God wanted him to become, even if that was to be a penniless Rabbi who taught people to be peacemakers and to love each other as God loves them instead of a pro-rich and violence-inducing religious figure.

Matthew's gospel says that after the angel came, Joseph opened himself up to the incredible possibilities of God. He took a positive view of the future, and it shaped the way Jesus grew up. Sometimes silence is important.

I vividly remember in college a pep talk my teammates and I received every year the day before we went home for Christmas. The head football coach would gather us players together in the gymnasium. "Men," he would begin, "Tomorrow you go home for Christmas. For God's sake, don't get in a fight with your parents or brothers and sisters. It is supposed to be a happy time. I don't want any phone calls this year from your parents. Keep silent when you think you are being treated like a 12 year old. Your family isn't used to having you around, staying out until all hours of the night with young people your age. Remember, it's their house. Bite your tongue, and keep your mouth shut. At least observe a truce until you get back here to the campus."

Warring cultures have historically observed uneasy truces during holiday seasons. The fighting Greek city-states would hold a truce for a few months when the Olympic Games were held every four years in Olympia or Delphi. On occasions during both world wars, Allied and German soldiers would sing to each other "Silent Night" across the cold, quiet battlefronts of Europe. In World War I, British troops even exchanged Christmas presents with their German enemies on Christmas Day. Then the next day, they returned to trying to kill each other. A truce is understandable. A truce is a lull between the fighting. A peace is something much more difficult to obtain than a truce.

The letter that Paul wrote to the church in Philippi doesn't begin like the beautiful gospel passages of sweet Virgin Mary and her older cousin Elizabeth getting along fabulously together in their time of pregnancy. Paul is *pleading* with two women in the church at Philippi to quit fighting. Paul is pleading for peace within the church. Like all good citizens then, as now, the Philippians understood truces, compromises, lawsuits, fights, and appearances. But peace was a mystery they had trouble with.

Jesus the Christ, like the prophets before Him, let forth the dream of a world of peace, where the will of God would be done. He preached about a kingdom of God where the lion would lie down with the lamb, where the king on the throne would be a Prince of Peace and not a totalitarian despot. He said his spirit, his Holy Spirit, would be here to support it.

The power of the presence of the spirit of God can be a wonderful thing. It can shape people's conduct. The Bible claims there can be a presence of Jesus Christ in our lives apart from our intelligence, the profession we are in, the company we work for, or the money we amass; and that presence can influence other people and our own life for genuine peace of mind, instead of an uneasy worldly truce.

As I look through the pages of the Bible, I'm amazed at the power of God's presence in the lives of particular persons to influence crowds and even whole nations. Moses goes up the mountain and meets with God. As he comes down, his face starts shining. Moses doesn't know that his face is glowing with the presence of God.

On further in the Bible, some palace guards throw a prophet named Daniel into a den full of lions. Then they pushed a great stone over the hole in the concrete where Daniel had been thrown. After a period of silence, they peeked down into the pit. There stood Daniel. And there stood the lions, dazed by a holy presence.

Then over in the New Testament, Peter and the other disciples are arrested. The religious leaders are trying to figure out why these guys are powerful. They see that these men didn't know everything. In fact, they see these disciples of Jesus as people who do not know correct grammar and are "idiots who didn't have great education." But they rightly assumed that their power is due not to their speech or their worldly power but to their "having been with Jesus."

It is amazing to me that Jesus lived on this earth for but 33 years at the most. According to three of the four gospel writers, Jesus and his disciples spent just one year living, traveling, and working together. The other gospel, John, claims it was three years. That is not much time.

If we were to take all the *unduplicated words of Jesus* left to us in the Bible and record them on a compact disk, do you know how long the CD would play? Forty-two minutes at the most. Jesus left us few words, yet Jesus has influenced countless millions. He apparently was not much of a shouter and even less of an arguer. He must have spent a lot of time just being there with folks. It was the presence of this loving person that influenced the crowd. His presence helped effect a revolution that could not be planned for, could not be researched and anticipated, and could not be purchased. As we look at our lives and our churches, what is it that gives us peace? If we take away the reading of the scriptures, the pontifications, the budgets, the study groups, the music, and the sermons, all of which are great and good, is there a peaceful presence of Jesus Christ there that guards our hearts and minds in this world of religious shouters and arguers?

God's presence in Jesus changed things. A man named Andrew went to his brother Simon one day. He said, "I think I've found him. Come and see." There was no manipulation to go hear a speech or watch a miracle. "Just come and see this Jesus. Come and be in his presence," Andrew said.

That's the same challenge that is given to us in our convoluted and complex world. Stand quietly strong and grant others the freedom to live their lives and relate to God in ways that may be different from the ways you relate to God. It takes a lot of faith to stand silent and trust in God and let God talk rather than you talking for God. But that may be the very essence of the Christian faith. May God grant us all the presence of Jesus, and may we grant to others the silent voice of our peace.

Broken Dreams And
Healed Hearts

— the lessons —

*Now on that same day two of them were going to a village called
Emmaus, about seven miles from Jerusalem, and talking with each
other about all these things that had happened. While they were talking
and discussing, Jesus himself came near and went with them, but their
eyes were kept from recognizing him. And he said to them, "What are
you discussing with each other while you walk along?" They stood still,
looking sad. Then one of them, whose name was Cleopas, answered him,
"Are you the only stranger in Jerusalem who does not know the things
that have taken place there in these days?" He asked them, "What
things?" They replied, "The things about Jesus of Nazareth, who was
a prophet mighty in deed and word before God and all the people, and
how our chief priests and leaders handed him over to be condemned
to death and crucified him. But we had hoped that he was the one
to redeem Israel.*

—Luke 24:13-21

*We know that all good things work together for good for those who
love God, who are called according to his purpose. For those whom he
foreknew he also predestined to be conformed to the image of his Son,
in order that he might be the firstborn within a large family. And those
whom he predestined he also called; and those whom he called he also
justified; and those whom he justified he also glorified.*

—Romans 8:28-30

D reams and visions can be beautiful things. Dreams and visions can also be very crushing. Many times, we invent certain images of the way life is supposed to be, and then we are somewhat shocked at the way things do not turn out.

The story is told of a raven, a common crow, which put on the clothes of an eagle. He broke into the eagle's world. He walked like an eagle. He flew with the eagles. He ate with the eagles. The eagles accepted him. But underneath, he always knew he was a crow in eagle's clothing. The higher he flew, the more afraid he became that the eagle costume would fall off, exposing him as the worthless crow he really was.

Dr. J. Wallace Hamilton, in his book *Horns and Halos in Human Nature*, tells of one of the weirdest auction sales in history. It was held in the city of Washington, D.C. It was an auction of designs and patent models of old inventions that did not make it in the marketplace. There were over 150,000 designs up for auction. Obviously, at one time, somebody had high hopes for each of those dreams that did not make it.[12] Some people died in poverty, having spent all their money trying to sell a dream that got exposed as worthless. One hundred fifty thousand dreams exposed as worthless.

If we call God the master designer of the universe, then we could view the New Testament as a book of broken dreams. It begins with a massacre of innocent children by King Herod. It is centered in the execution of its hero, Jesus Christ. And it ends with the martyred saints crying, "How long, O Lord, how long must we wait for your return?" In terms of the design of life, the crucifixion of Jesus caused serious questions to be written in the minds of humanity. There, on the cross, was a man who loved his enemies, a man whose righteousness was greater than the Pharisees, a man who was rich but became poor, a man who gave his robe to those who took his cloak, a man who prayed for those who despitefully used him.13 Yet, society crucified him, executed him. The question to ask in the presence of this horrific scene is whether goodness is the design of the universe or is exposed as worthless. Is religion a bunch of smoke and mirrors? Does God's design really pay off?

We perhaps can identify with the men on the road to Emmaus who were walking and talking with each other. They told of all that had happened—how this Jesus of Nazareth, mighty in deed and word before God and all the people, had been condemned to death and crucified.

Are there any clearer words of a broken dream than theirs? "But we had hoped he was the one to redeem Israel." (Luke 24:21). We had hoped he was the one to make it. We had dreamed he would be the one. But it just didn't work out. It was all smoke and mirrors. The costume fell off, and the eagle turned out to be a crow in disguise.

Sometimes you and I have our dreams fall apart. We come back home with a broken dream in our hip pocket, a sure-fire program that fell flat, a preventative that didn't prevent, a solution that did not solve, a panacea that did not pan out, a pill that did not work, or a surgery that could not get it all. We wail the plaintive cry, "But I had hoped this would redeem me. Oh, I had hoped it would be another way."

It has been very well said that *every person dreams of one life and is forced to live another.* Such appears to have been true for Jesus, and yes, even for God! From the Garden of Eden to the Crucifixion, God seems to have had a grand dream for the human race but was forced to live another experience. Apparently, even God dreamed of one kind of life and was forced to live another.

All of us dream of one kind of life and are frequently forced to live another. Here, it seems, is the essence of life. If, indeed, every person dreams of one life and is ultimately forced to live another, then the manner in which one repairs that dream has to be the greatest news in the world. The essence of the crucifixion and the resurrection of Jesus Christ are not solely to be found in a personal guarantee of life after death for you and me. The resurrection of Christ is an affirmation of certain goodness in life. The schematic designs of human evil were exposed and condemned for what they were. The central claim of the New Testament is the ultimate triumph of goodness.

Consequently, St. Paul could affirm, "And we know that all things work together for good to them that love God, to them who are called according to God's dream." (Romans 8:28). Here, Paul is not saying that we all get to live the life of our dreams. A lot of things happen to us that are *not good.* Paul *is* saying that if a person will consider all the experiences of his or her life, both the good and the bad, and bond them together with love for God, then the sum total of that life will be good. As such, it is indeed possible to believe in the sun when it is not shining, to believe in love when you cannot directly feel it, and to believe in God when God is silent for a period. Even if the world crucifies you, the design of God's universe and your life with it will ultimately triumph.

If God's dream for goodness triumphs, then one thing is certain: Failure is relative to time. No one really knows when he or she has succeeded or failed if all he does is look at the present.[14] God's design and God's time turn a lot of failures into successes.

Consider the case of a little girl named Sadako Sasaki. When she was but a toddler, her hometown of Hiroshima, Japan, was targeted to be destroyed by an atomic bomb at the end of World War II. One day, a yellow flash came. A powerful blast of wind and fire destroyed the city. Nearly 100,000 human beings were killed instantly. Those few who lived contracted what was then called the A-bomb sickness. Today we call it leukemia, a deadly form of cancer. Sadako lived with leukemia for 11 years and was constantly in and out of the Hiroshima Red Cross Hospital. She folded over 1,000 paper cranes and continued folding them, hoping for recovery because of a popular Japanese belief that says, "Folding 1,000 paper cranes will bring good luck." But her hope was not immediately realized. Naked, bleeding, hairless, and with skin hanging loose, she died in the fall of 1955 when she was 12 years old. She believed in love when she could not feel it, and she believed in God when God appeared to be silent. She dreamed of one life and was forced to live another.

Some of her fellow schoolmates went to see her the week she died. They saw the wistful dream on her face as she folded the paper cranes. One of them, a child named Yamaguchi, said, "Let's erect a monument by ourselves to comfort Sadako's soul and appeal for peace against the cruelty of war." Obviously, it would cost a lot of money. But the children decided to put aside money from their allowances. Other children heard of the effort, and on January 28, 1956, a meeting was held in which every school in Hiroshima sent a delegate. They decided to raise money for a "Children's Peace Monument" in honor of Sadako.

Soon children all over the world were sending in their pennies for it. It took 32 years for Sadako's broken dream to get put back together. In 1988, the Children's Peace Monument was unveiled. It is the figure of two children on either side and another child on top, their arms outstretched to reveal their hope for a peaceful world. It is the largest monument to peace in the history of the world. So many Japanese children kept the center of that statue filled with thousands of multi-colored paper cranes that the Japanese government had to build, and to this day still maintains, a dozen glass sheds to protect the hundreds of thousands of multi-colored cranes that are brought by Japanese school children each month.

God's design of love holds. It stands. It triumphs for all generations over any design of darkness and death. Paul is absolutely correct. History has proved it in a thousand ways. If a person will consider all the experiences of his life, and bond them together with love for God, then the sum total of that life will be good. I am always amazed at the persistence and effort people put into life to affirm and receive the goodness of God.

I myself have seen incredible good come that most frightening of all historical moments. Before coming to High Point to live, I was fortunate to have as an administrative assistant, a young Japanese woman named Ruiko Kuwabara Connor, a brilliant and dedicated lady. Ruiko's father, Toichiro Kuwabara, was an amazing man. I marveled at his generosity and warm human spirit the few times that I got to be with him. On the day the atomic bomb was dropped on Hiroshima, he was a 25-year-old ophthalmologist teaching at the University of Kyushu in Japan.

Not long after Hiroshima was destroyed, the Atomic Energy Commission of the United States sent doctors to Japan to study the effects of radiation on people. Dr. Kuwabara worked with them. They treated masses of people whose eyes were blinded and burned by radiation, something we pray will never occur again. In 1952, one of the American doctors, a professor from Harvard Medical School, persuaded Dr. Kuwabara to come to the United States to live and work. His family, consisting of his wife and two little girls, joined him two years later.

Dr. Kuwabara became a faculty member of the Harvard Medical School and worked in the Howe Laboratory of the Massachusetts Eye and Ear Infirmary for 30 years, earning the rank of Professor of Pathology in the National Eye Institute.

Author of more than 250 references, he was one of the most widely cited ophthalmologists in history. Dr. Kuwabara was also a pioneer in applying electron and scanning electron microscopy to the eye. He has, perhaps, done as much to prevent blindness as any other human being.

After I left Cambridge, his daughter Ruiko became the Grants Coordinator of the Reischauer Institute of Japanese Studies at Harvard. Her primary purpose was administrative coordination of the post-doctoral fellowships and grants for students in all fields of Japanese studies. Much of her generosity, effectiveness, and all around spirit of helpfulness, I have no doubt, were instilled by her father, Dr. Kuwabara. His relationship with her and her sister evidenced his profound commitment to ethics and the hope for a better world. When they first arrived in America, and throughout their childhood, Dr. Kuwabara taught his daughters English by reading to them each night a few pages from the Hebrew prophets in the Old Testament and from *The Diary of Anne Frank*. He also took his family to tour the World War II death camps in Germany and Poland. A man of few words, he seldom talked about his experiences in that War, but he often repeated to his children, "How could mankind do this to one another?"[15]

There are so many people who believed in love when they could not feel it and believed in God when God appeared to be silent. They stand as living examples that the master design of the moral universe, though battered and wounded, will not stay down. When I become discouraged about the troubles I encounter in life, it soothes my soul to think of a renowned physician who was born in a Buddhist country and who saw human destruction at its worst sitting down at night to teach his little girls a new language through reading the Hebrew prophets and the story of Anne Frank. That is a language most of our world has yet to learn. Another great physician, from Nazareth, thousands of years ago, claimed to have come to make the blind see again. He asked, "Why do you have eyes to see, but do not see?" Then, this one called Jesus showed us how a healed heart can enable us to see beyond the broken dreams of humanity into a kingdom of peace and joy where the lion and the lamb sleep together.

I believe that the design of God will ultimately triumph in spite of some of our human mistakes and broken dreams. From Bethlehem to Gethsemane to Calvary, to Hiroshima to Auschwitz, to the present day, the innocent do suffer. The good and the lonely often get what they do not deserve. But goodness never stays in the dark. The truth never stays crucified. The central theme in human history is the same as the central theme of the New Testament: the ultimate triumph of goodness. Broken dreams can be turned into healed hearts. Take comfort. Have courage. Recover your peace of mind.

— end notes —

PART ONE

[1] Harry Emerson Fosdick, *Dear Mister Brown: Letters To A Person Perplexed About Religion* (New York: Harper and Row Publishers, 1961), p. 41. The quote from De Tocqueville and the date relative to India, Wal-Mart, and Google can be found in the article, "Two cheers for America," July 4th-10th 2009 issue of *The Economist*, p. 30.

[2] This material comes from Eric Metaxas, *Amazing Grace: William Wilberforce and the Heroic Campaign to End Slavery* (San Francisco: HarperSanFrancisco, 2007), especially pp. xv-xviii.

[3] Chuck Yeager and Leo Janos, *Yeager: An Autobiography*. New York: Bantam Books, 1986.

[4] See "Question marks," *The Economist*, June 7, 2008, p. 95. The article is a review of *The Man Who Loved China: The Fantastic Story of the Eccentric Scientist Who Unlocked the Mysteries of the Middle Kingdom.*, by Simon Winchester, Harper Collins, 2008.

[5] The story of Frank Boreham is told by Robert Cleveland Holland in *Robert Holland at Shadyside* (Pittsburgh: The Shadyside Presbyterian Church, 1985), pp. 25-31. The analysis of the story and its use in this context are my own. It is interesting to note that in Tibetan Buddhism and Japanese Shintoism, the dog is an object of worship. In fact, in Japan, two dogs are placed in front of Shinto temples to drive away evil spirits.

[6] George A. Buttrick, ed., *The Interpreter's Bible, Volume X* (New York: Abingdon, 1953), p. 334.

[7] Margery Williams, *The Velveteen Rabbit or How Toys Become Real*. (Garden City, NY: Doubleday and Company, 1922).

[8] Taken from Jack Pennington, West Hills Baptist Church, Knoxville, Tennessee. Jack used the illustration in a sermon, "Ambassadors for Christ."

[9] Peter J. Gomes, *Yet More Sundays at Harvard* (Cambridge, Massachusetts: The Memorial Church, 1997), p. 103.

PART TWO

[1] Archbishop William Keeler, "A Tale of Two Cities," opening address to the National Conference of Catholic Bishops, November 15, 1993, Washington, D.C.

[2] See Bruce Larson, *There's A Lot More To Health Than Not Being Sick* (Waco, Texas: Word, Inc., 1981), p. 20.

[3] *Ibid*, p. 132.

[4] *The Green Pastures* was first produced at the Mansfield Theatre, New York City, by Laurence Rivers, Inc., on February 26, 1930 and closed on August 29, 1931. Marc Connelly's original play may be found in *Sixteen Famous American Plays*, edited by Bennet Cerf and Van H. Cartwell (Garden City, New York: Garden City Publishing Co., 1941). It was produced in many versions. I have used a combination of the original and later productions, trying to retain the meaning and purpose of the original while fitting some of the language into my sermon.

[5] *Ibid*

[6] Donald Caskie, *The Tartan Pimpernel* (Edinburgh: Birlinn Limited, 1999), pp. 223-224.

[7] Among many that quote this event is Chuck Swindoll in *Growing Strong in the Seasons of Life* (Grand Rapids, Michigan: Zondervan, 1994), pp. 50-51.

[8] The Associated Press. My attention was drawn to the story by reading Robert G. Hall, *Singing the Lord's Song* (Greenwood, SC: Drinkard Litho. 2003), p. 128.

[9] Clyde Foushee, *Animated Object Talks* (Old Tappan, NJ: Fleming H. Revell, 1956), p. 13.

PART THREE

[1] See the note for Acts 19:9 in the New Revised Standard Version of the Bible. One of the better commentaries on the passage is that of John Calvin, *Calvin's Commentaries: The Acts of the Apostles, 14-28*, translated by John W. Fraser (Grand Rapids: Wm. B. Eerdmans Publishing Company, 1966), p. 154. Calvin's Commentary on Acts first appeared in 1554.

[2] Lawrence Cunningham and John Kelsey, *The Sacred Quest: An Invitation to the Study of Religion* (Upper Saddle River, New Jersey: Prentice Hall, 2002), pp. 8-9. Robert Cummings Neville, *The God Who Beckons: Theology in the Form of Sermons* (Nashville: Abingdon Press, 1999), pp. 103-105.

[3] The illustration is used in John R. Steward, *Tales for the Pulpit* (Lima, Ohio: CSS Publishing, 1997), p. 37.

[4] For the material on King Philip's War see the incisive book, by Nathan Philbrick, *Mayflower: A Story of Courage, Community, and War* (New York: Viking, 2006), especially the preface.

[5] Luke placed the story in Galilee in the home of Simon, a Pharisee. See for more information: James Harnish, *Radical Renovation* (Nashville: Abingdon Press, 2008), pp. 45-46.

[6] Mark Trotter, "Dig In," First United Methodist Church, San Diego, California, October 25, 1998, p. 2.

[7] This story was originally told by Warren Buffet in a speech given at New York Society of Security Analysts, December 6, 1994. It is quoted in the book by Janet Lowe, *Warren Buffet Speaks--Revised* (Hoboken, New Jersey: John Wiley and Sons, 2007), p. 93.

[8] Richard Shenkman, *Legends, Lies, and Myths* (New York: William Morrow and Company, 1988), p. 84.

[9] Winona Laduke, "We Are Still Here," *Sojourners* (October, 1991), p. 12.

[10] Harold Cooke Phillips, "Closing the Door," in *Sunday Evening Sermons*, edited by Alton M. Motter (New York: Harper), p. 91. Phillips became the pastor of First Baptist Church of Cleveland in 1928. The church is now First Baptist Church of Greater Cleveland. This book of edited sermons, is fifteen sermons preached to the Sunday Evening Association in Chicago.

PART FOUR

[1] Warren C. Hamby, *Winds of Change* (Old Tappan, NJ: Fleming H. Revell, 1971), pp. 74-75.

[2] See Joseph R. Jeter, Jr., pp. 30-31, and Amanda J. Burr, pp. 91-96 for two excellent sermons on Revelation 6 in Cornish R. Rogers and Joseph R. Jeter, Jr., (eds.) *Preaching Through the Apocalypse* (St. Louis: Chalice Press, 1992).

[3] Amanda J. Burr, "Now That's A Horse Of A Different Color!" pp. 91-96, *Preaching Through the Apocalypse*. Ms. Burr is pastor of the First Christian Church of Reseda, California.

[4] Paul Aurandt, *Destiny* (New York: William Morrow and Company, 1983), pp. 142-43.

[5] *Ibid.*

[6] See two salient articles: "Land of the Free?" p. 44 in the May 10, 2008, edition of *The Economist* and "Compassionate centrism," in the October 13, 2007, edition of *The Economist*. Both articles were written by British journalists looking at the United States. The data is from those articles. The focus on self-correcting is my own trajectory.

[7] See the above mentioned article, "Compassionate centrism."

[8] Marva J. Dawn, *Unfettered Hope: A Call to Faithful Living in an Affluent Society.* (Louisville: Westminster John Knox Press, 2006), p. xvii.

[9] James Gordon Gilkey, *How To Be Your Best* (New York: The Macmillan Company, 1942), pp. 128-129.

[10] G. Curtis Jones, *Which Way Is Progress?* (Saint Louis: Bethany Press, 1953), pp. 30-31.

PART FIVE

[1] Harold E. Kohn, *Pathways to Understanding* (Grand Rapids: Eerdmans, 1958), p. 147.

[2] Robert Farr Capron, *An Offering of Uncles* (New York: Sheed and Ward, 1967), p. 115.

[3] Craig Lambert, "The Science of Happiness," *Harvard Magazine*, January-February, 2007, pp. 26-30, 94.

[4] This story was told by Marcus Bach, *Let Life Be Like This* (Englewood Cliffs: Prentice-Hall, 1963), pp. 7-8.

[5] *Ibid*

[6] There are many sources coming to light about the life of Adolph Sannwald. See the book by Peter J. Gomes, *The Scandalous Gospel of Jesus* (New York: Harper-Collins, 2007), pp. 71-72, and articles written in The *Harvard Crimson*, 2002 and 2003.

[7] See the aforementioned article written by Malcolm C. Young, Rector of Christ Episcopal Church, in *Los Alamos Town Crier*, April 23, 2008.

[8] Peter J. Gomes, *The Scandalous Gospel of Jesus* (New York: Harper-Collins, 2007), pp. 71-72.

[9] Greg Mortenson and David Oliver Relin, *Three Cups of Tea: One Man's Mission to Promote Peace . . . One School at a Time.* (New York: Viking Press, 2006), see especially p. 150.

[10] See Harold A. Bosley, *Preaching on Controversial Issues.* (New York: Harper, 1953), pp. 68-69.

[11] William Beebe, *The Arcturus Adventure*, p. 111. Beebe is quoted by James Gordon Gilkey in *Managing One's Self.* (New York: The Macmillan Company, 1936).

[12] As used by Charles L. Allen in *The Miracle of Hope* (Old Tappan, N.J.: Fleming H. Revell Co., 1983), pp. 16-17.

[13] See John Howard Yoder, *The Politics of Jesus* (Grand Rapids, Minn.: Wm. B. Eerdmans, 1972), p. 61.

[14] Ernest A. Fitzgerald, *How To Be A Successful Failure* (New York: Atheneum, 1978), pp. 6-8.

[15] The information on Dr.Kuwabara was developed from academic research and personal conversations and e-mails with Ruiko K. Connor and Tim Connor, who still reside in Cambridge, Massachusetts, as of this writing. I am greatly in debt to them for their correspondence and editing for accuracy the initial drafts of chapter 30. For additional information, see David G. Coogan, "Toichiro Kuwabara 1920-1991," *American Journal of Ophthalmology, Vol. 112, No. 1,* July 15, 1991, pp. 107-108.